Networking Essentials Version 3: Cisco Certified Support Technician (CCST) Networking 100-150

Lab Manual

Cisco Networking Academy

Cisco Press

Hoboken, NJ 07030

Networking Essentials Version 3: Cisco Certified Support Technician (CCST) Networking 100-150 Lab Manual

Cisco Networking Academy

Copyright© 2024 Cisco Systems, Inc.

Published by:
Cisco Press
Hoboken, NJ 07030

2 2024

Library of Congress Control Number: 2023915721

ISBN-13: 978-0-13-829372-7
ISBN-10: 0-13-829372-4

Vice President, IT Professional
Mark Taub

Director, Product Line Management
Brett Bartow

Alliance Manager, Cisco Press
Jaci Featherly
James Risler

Executive Editor
James Manly

Managing Editor
Sandra Schroeder

Senior Project Editor
Mandie Frank

Editorial Assistant
Cindy Teeters

Designer
Chuti Prasertsith

Compositor
codeMantra

Proofreader
Rick Kughen

CISCO.

Warning and Disclaimer

This book is designed to provide information about networking. Every effort has been made to make this book as complete and as accurate as possible, but no warranty or fitness is implied.

The information is provided on an "as is" basis. The authors, Cisco Press, and Cisco Systems, Inc. shall have neither liability nor responsibility to any person or entity with respect to any loss or damages arising from the information contained in this book or from the use of the discs or programs that may accompany it.

The opinions expressed in this book belong to the author and are not necessarily those of Cisco Systems, Inc.

Trademark Acknowledgments

All terms mentioned in this book that are known to be trademarks or service marks have been appropriately capitalized. Cisco Press or Cisco Systems, Inc., cannot attest to the accuracy of this information. Use of a term in this book should not be regarded as affecting the validity of any trademark or service mark.

This book is part of the Cisco Networking Academy" series from Cisco Press. The products in this series support and complement the Cisco Networking Academy curriculum. For more information on the Cisco Networking Academy or to locate a Networking Academy, please visit netacad.com.

Special Sales

For information about buying this title in bulk quantities, or for special sales opportunities (which may include electronic versions; custom cover designs; and content particular to your business, training goals, marketing focus, or branding interests), please contact our corporate sales department at corpsales@pearsoned.com or (800) 382-3419.

For government sales inquiries, please contact governmentsales@pearson.com

For questions about sales outside the U.S., please contact intlcs@pearson.com

Feedback Information

At Cisco Press, our goal is to create in-depth technical books of the highest quality and value. Each book is crafted with care and precision, undergoing rigorous development that involves the unique expertise of members from the professional technical community.

Readers' feedback is a natural continuation of this process. If you have any comments regarding how we could improve the quality of this book, or otherwise alter it to better suit your needs, you can contact us through email at feedback@ciscopress.com. Please make sure to include the book title and ISBN in your message.

We greatly appreciate your assistance.

CISCO

Americas Headquarters	Asia Pacific Headquarters	Europe Headquarters
Cisco Systems, Inc.	Cisco Systems (USA) Pte. Ltd.	Cisco Systems International BV Amsterdam,
San Jose, CA	Singapore	The Netherlands

Cisco has more than 200 offices worldwide. Addresses, phone numbers, and fax numbers are listed on the Cisco Website at **www.cisco.com/go/offices**.

Cisco and the Cisco logo are trademarks or registered trademarks of Cisco and/or its affiliates in the U.S. and other countries. To view a list of Cisco trademarks, go to this URL: www.cisco.com/go/trademarks. Third party trademarks mentioned are the property of their respective owners. The use of the word partner does not imply a partnership relationship between Cisco and any other company. (1110R)

Pearson's Commitment to Diversity, Equity, and Inclusion

Pearson is dedicated to creating bias-free content that reflects the diversity of all learners. We embrace the many dimensions of diversity, including but not limited to race, ethnicity, gender, socioeconomic status, ability, age, sexual orientation, and religious or political beliefs.

Education is a powerful force for equity and change in our world. It has the potential to deliver opportunities that improve lives and enable economic mobility. As we work with authors to create content for every product and service, we acknowledge our responsibility to demonstrate inclusivity and incorporate diverse scholarship so that everyone can achieve their potential through learning. As the world's leading learning company, we have a duty to help drive change and live up to our purpose to help more people create a better life for themselves and to create a better world.

Our ambition is to purposefully contribute to a world where:

- Everyone has an equitable and lifelong opportunity to succeed through learning.

- Our educational products and services are inclusive and represent the rich diversity of learners.

- Our educational content accurately reflects the histories and experiences of the learners we serve.

- Our educational content prompts deeper discussions with learners and motivates them to expand their own learning (and worldview).

While we work hard to present unbiased content, we want to hear from you about any concerns or needs with this Pearson product so that we can investigate and address them.

- Please contact us with concerns about any potential bias at https://www.pearson.com/report-bias.html.

Table of Contents

About This Lab Manual

This is the only authorized Lab Manual for the Cisco Networking Academy Networking Essentials Course.

Networking is at the heart of the digital transformation. The network is essential to many business functions today, including business-critical data and operations, cybersecurity, and so much more. A wide variety of career paths rely on the network—so it's important to understand what the network can do, how it operates, and how to protect it.

This is a great course for developers, data scientists, cybersecurity specialists, and other professionals looking to broaden their networking domain knowledge. It's also an excellent launching point for students pursuing a wide range of career pathways—from cybersecurity to software development to business and more. A Networking Academy digital badge is available for the instructor-led version of this course. No prerequisites are required.

You'll learn these core skills:

- Plan and install a home or small business network using wireless technology, then connect it to the internet.

- Develop critical thinking and problem-solving skills using Cisco Packet Tracer.

- Practice verifying and troubleshooting network and Internet connectivity.

- Recognize and mitigate security threats to a home network. The 37 comprehensive labs in this manual emphasize hands-on learning and practice to reinforce configuration skills.

The Networking Essentials Lab Manual provides you with all the labs and packet tracer activity instructions from the course designed as hands-on practice to develop critical thinking and complex problem-solving skills.

Command Syntax Conventions

The conventions used to present command syntax in this book are the same conventions used in the IOS Command Reference. The Command Reference describes these conventions as follows:

- **Boldface** indicates commands and keywords that are entered literally as shown. In actual configuration examples and output (not general command syntax), boldface indicates commands that are manually input by the user (such as a **show** command).

- *Italic* indicates arguments for which you supply actual values.

- Vertical bars (|) separate alternative, mutually exclusive elements.

- Square brackets ([ ]) indicate an optional element.

- Braces ({ }) indicate a required choice.

- Braces within brackets ([{ }]) indicate a required choice within an optional element.

Communication in a Connected World

This chapter contains no labs or packet tracers.

Network Components, Types, and Connections

This chapter contains no labs or packet tracers.

Wireless and Mobile Networks

This chapter contains no labs or packet tracers.

4.4.4. Packet Tracer–Configure a Wireless Router and Clients

Objectives

- Part 1: Connect the Devices
- Part 2: Configure the Wireless Router
- Part 3: Configure IP Addressing and Test Connectivity

Background / Scenario

Your friend, Natsumi, heard that you are studying networking. She asked you to come over and help her connect her new home to the cable TV network. You need to connect the correct cables to the correct devices, connect devices to a home wireless router, and configure the router to provide IP addresses to network clients. Natsumi also wants you to set up a wireless LAN for her home network, so you will configure that as well. You are confident that this will be an easy process, and the network will be set up in no time.

Instructions

Part 1: Connect the Devices

The work area shows the interior of your friend's house. Scroll the window to get a sense of the layout of the house and the location of the devices. In this part, you will connect all the labeled devices.

Step 1: Connect the coaxial cables.

Natsumi's cable company delivers internet and video services to her home through a coaxial cable. The cable is connected to an outlet in her home. A splitter device separates the internet data service from the video service. This enables the two services to be connected to the appropriate devices. You will connect the internet service to the cable modem and the video service to the television.

a. In **Network Components**, click **Connections** (the lightning bolt).

b. Locate and click the **Coaxial** cable icon. It is the blue zigzag icon.

c. Click **Cable Splitter** and select the **Coaxial1** port.

d. Click **Cable Modem** and select **Port 0**.

e. Repeat the previous steps to connect **Coaxial2** on the **Cable Splitter** to **Port 0** on the **TV**.

f.   Click the **TV** and then click **ON** for **Status**. If your connections are correct, you should see an image appear that represents a TV program.

Step 2: Connect the network cables.

There are two PCs in Natsumi's house. They don't have wireless LAN adapters, so they will be connected with Ethernet cables. The home wireless router is the center of the network. It enables devices that are configured on the home network to communicate with each other and the internet. The router includes a network switch that accepts wired connections for up to four hosts. You will connect the PCs to these ports.

For the **Home Wireless Router** to access the internet over the cable TV provider network, the cable modem must be connected to the home wireless router internet port. This is done with a copper straight-through cable.

a.   Click **Connections** and then **Copper Straight-Through** cable. It looks like a solid black line.

b.   Connect **Port 1** on the **Cable Modem** to the **Internet** port of the **Home Wireless Router**.

c.   Click the **Office PC** and connect the cable to the **FastEthernet0** port. Locate the **Home Wireless Router** and click it. Connect the other end of the cable to the **GigabitEthernet 1** port to complete the connection.

d.   Repeat the previous steps to connect the **Bedroom PC** to the **GigabitEthernet 2** port on the **Home Wireless Router**.

The wired home network is now fully connected to the internet through the cable TV provider network.

Part 2: Configure the Wireless Router

Most home wireless routers are configured by using a graphical user interface (GUI) that is accessed through your computer's web browser. In this part, you will access the home wireless router through the browser on the **Office PC** and configure Natsumi's home network.

Step 1: Access the home wireless router GUI.

a.   Click the **Office PC > Desktop** tab, and then **IP Configuration**.

b.   Click **DHCP**. DHCP will automatically configure the **Office PC** to be on the same IP network as the **Home Wireless Router**.

c.   After a brief delay, the values for the **IP Configuration** should automatically update. The IPv4 address should start with the number 192. If it does not, click **Fast Forward Time**, which is just below the network topology in the lower left-hand corner. This will speed up the simulation of DHCP.

d.   Make note of the address for the default gateway. The default gateway is the device that provides devices on the home network with access to outside networks, such as the internet. In this case, the default gateway address is the address of the **Home Wireless Router**.

e.   Keeping the **Office PC** window open, close the **IP Configuration** window, and then click **Web Browser**. Enter the IP address of the **Home Wireless Router** (the default gateway address) into the **URL** box and click **Go**.

f. Newly installed home routers are configured with default credentials. Enter **admin** for both the **User Name** and **Password**. You should now see the GUI for the **Home Wireless Router** appear; you are ready to configure Natsumi's network. Adjust the window size as necessary to see more of the interface.

Note: Default passwords on real-world devices should be changed immediately because it is widely known, including by threat actors.

Step 2: Configure basic settings.

In this step, you will configure a new username and password for the wireless router and limit the number of IP addresses that DHCP will issue to hosts connected to the network.

Natsumi only has a few devices that will connect to the network, and she will not have a lot of friends visiting. She thinks no more than 10 devices would connect to her network at any one time. You decide to lower the number of users to 10. Your friend lives in a densely populated part of town, so it is possible many people could see her wireless network.

a. You are currently viewing configuration options under the **Setup** tab. Locate the **Network Setup** area. This is where you can configure the router's DHCP server settings. Locate the **Maximum Number of Users** field; enter **10**. Scroll down to the bottom of the page and click **Save Settings**. You must save settings on every page of the GUI in which you make changes.

Note: It is possible you will lose your connection to the router. Click **Go** in the web browser to reload the GUI page. You may need to close the **Web Browser**; click **IP Configuration**, and toggle between **DHCP** and **Static** to refresh the IP addressing for **Office PC**. Then verify the **Office PC** has an IP address configuration that starts with 192. Open the **Web Browser** again, enter the router's IP address, and re-authenticate with **admin** as the default credentials.

---

b. Click the **Administration** tab. Here, you can change the default **admin** password. Enter and confirm **MyPassword1!** as the new password. Scroll to the bottom of the page and click **Save Settings**.

You will be prompted to log in again. Enter **admin** as the **User Name** and **MyPassword1!** as the new password, and the click **Continue**.

Step 3: Configure a wireless LAN.

At this point, you are ready to configure Natsumi's wireless network so she can connect her wireless devices to the internet over Wi-Fi.

a. Scroll back to the top of the window and then click the **Wireless** tab.

b. For the **2.4 GHz** network, click **Enable** to activate the network radio.

c. Change the **Network Name (SSID)** from **Default** to **MyHome**. When people look for Wi-Fi networks to connect to, they will see this network name. The network name can be hidden, but this can make it a little harder for guests to connect to the network. Scroll to the bottom of the page and click **Save Settings**.

d. Now you will configure security on the **MyHome** network. This will prevent unauthorized people from connecting to the wireless network. Scroll back to the top of the window, and then click **Wireless Security** on the **Wireless** tab.

   e. Notice that security is currently disabled on all three wireless networks. You are only using the **2.4 GHz** network. Click the dropdown menu for the **2.4 GHz** network and select **WPA2 Personal**. This is the strongest security that this router offers for wireless networks.

   f. More settings are revealed. WPA2 Personal requires a passphrase that must be entered by anyone who wants to connect to the wireless network. Enter **MyPassPhrase1!** as the **Passphrase**. Note that capitalization is important.

   g. Scroll to the bottom of the page and click **Save Settings** and close the **Web Browser** for the Office PC.

Part 3: Configure IP Addressing and Test Connectivity

Now that the router is configured, in this part, you will configure IP addressing for the PCs and laptop and verify that they can connect to the internet.

Step 1: Connect the laptop to the wireless network.

   a. Click the **Laptop** in the living room, and then click the **Desktop** tab and select **PC Wireless**.

   b. Click the **Connect** tab. After a short delay the wireless network that you configured previously appear in the list of wireless network names.

   c. Click the name of the network that you created, and then click the **Connect** button.

   d. Enter the passphrase you configured earlier for the wireless network in the **Pre-shared Key** field, and then click **Connect**.

   e. Click the **Link Information** tab. You should see the message: **You have successfully connected to the access point.**

   f. Click the **More Information** button to see details about the connection. If the IP address does not begin with **192**, click **Fast Forward Time** several times to speed up the simulation.

   g. Close the **PC Wireless** app and open the **Web Browser**. Verify that the **Laptop** can now connect to **skillsforall.srv**, clicking **Fast Forward Time** until the page loads. This verifies that the **Laptop** has internet connectivity.

Step 2: Test connectivity from the Office PC.

You know that the Office PC can connect to the network because you used it to configure the router. However, can it also access the internet? If it can, then you will know that the wired network is properly connected and configured.

   a. Click **Office PC > Desktop** tab > **Web Browser**.

   b. Enter **skillsforall.srv** and click **Go**. After a brief delay, you should see the webpage appear. If necessary, click **Fast Forward Time** several times to speed up the convergence.

       Loading an external website verifies that internet connectivity for the **Office PC**.

Step 3: Configure the bedroom PC.

    a. For the **Bedroom PC**, open **IP Configuration** and set it to **DHCP**. Verify that the Bedroom PC received an IP address that begins with **192**.

    b. Close the **IP Configuration** window and open the **Web Browser**. Verify that the **Bedroom PC** can now connect to **skillsforall.srv**, clicking **Fast Forward Time** until the page loads. This verifies that the **Bedroom PC** has internet connectivity.

    You have now completed connecting network devices, configuring the router and wireless LAN, and configuring hosts to connect to the network. All devices should be able to connect to the internet. Your job is done, and Natsumi has offered to cook dinner for you as a reward for your help.

Communication Principles

This chapter contains no labs or packet tracers.

Network Media

This chapter contains no labs or packet tracers.

The Access Layer

This chapter contains no labs or packet tracers.

The Internet Protocol

Packet Tracer
☐ Activity

8.1.2 Packet Tracer—Connect to a Web Server

Objectives

- Observe how packets are sent across the Internet using IP addresses.

Instructions

Part 1: Verify Connectivity to the Web Server

a. Open the source host command prompt window. Select **PC0**.

b. Select the **Desktop** tab > **Command Prompt**.

c. Verify connectivity to the web server. At the command prompt, ping the IP address of the web server by entering **ping 172.33.100.50**.

```
PC> ping 172.33.100.50


Pinging 172.33.100.50 with 32 bytes of data:


Reply from 172.33.100.50: bytes=32 time=0ms TTL=127
Reply from 172.33.100.50: bytes=32 time=0ms TTL=127
Reply from 172.33.100.50: bytes=32 time=0ms TTL=127
Reply from 172.33.100.50: bytes=32 time=0ms TTL=127


Ping statistics for 172.33.100.50:
Packets: Sent = 4, Received = 3, Lost = 1 (25% loss),
Approximate round trip times in milli-seconds:
Minimum = 0ms, Maximum = 0ms, Average = 0ms
```

A reply verifies connectivity from the client to the destination web server. The reply may time out initially while devices load and ARP is performed.

d. Close the command prompt window only by clicking the **X** on the command prompt window. Be sure to leave the PC0 configuration window open.

Part 2: Connect to the Web Server via the Web Client

a. On the **Desktop** tab on PC0, select **Web Browser**.

b. Enter **172.33.100.50** as the **URL** and click **Go**. The web client will connect to the web server via the IP address and open the web page.

Question:

What messages did you see after the web page has finished loading?

_____

IPv4 and Network Segmentation

This chapter contains no labs or packet tracers.

CHAPTER 10

IPv6 Addressing Formats and Rules

This chapter contains no labs or packet tracers.

Dynamic Addressing with DHCP

Packet Tracer
☐ Activity

11.2.3 Packet Tracer–Configure DHCP on a Wireless Router

Objectives

- Connect three PCs to a wireless router
- Change the DHCP setting to a specific network range
- Configure the clients to obtain their address via DHCP

Background / Scenario

A home user wants to use a wireless router to connect three PCs. All three PCs should obtain their address automatically from the wireless router.

Instructions

Part 1: Set Up the Network Topology

a. Add three generic PCs.

b. Connect each PC to an Ethernet port on the wireless router using straight-through cables.

Part 2: Observe the Default DHCP Settings

a. After the amber lights have turned green, click **PC0**. Click the **Desktop** tab. Select **IP Configuration**. Select **DHCP** to receive an IP address from **DHCP Enabled Router**.

Question:

Record the IP address of the default gateway:

_____

b. Close the **IP Configuration** window.

c. Open a web browser.

d. Enter the IP address of the default gateway recorded earlier into the **URL** field. When prompted, enter the username **admin** and password **admin**.

e. Scroll through the **Basic Setup** page to view default settings, including the default IP address of the wireless router.

f. Notice that DHCP is enabled; this is the starting address of the DHCP range and the range of addresses available to clients.

Part 3: Change the Default IP Address of the Wireless Router

a. In the **Router IP Settings** section, change the IP address to **192.168.5.1**.

b. Scroll to the bottom of the page and click **Save Settings**.

c. If it is done correctly, the web page will display an error message. Close the web browser.

d. Click **IP Configuration** to renew the assigned IP address. Click **Static**. Click **DHCP** to receive new IP address information from the wireless router.

e. Open the web browser and enter the IP address **192.168.5.1** in the URL field. When prompted, enter the username **admin** and password **admin**.

Part 4: Change the Default DHCP Range of Addresses

a. Notice the DHCP Server Start IP Address is updated to the same network as the Router IP.

b. Change the **Starting IP Address** from 192.168.5.100 to **192.168.5.126**.

c. Change the **Maximum Number** of Users to **75**.

d. Scroll to the bottom of the page and click **Save Settings**. Close the web browser.

e. Click **IP Configuration** to renew the assigned IP address. Click **Static**. Click **DHCP** to receive new IP address information from the wireless router.

f. Select **Command Prompt**. Enter **ipconfig**.

Question:

Record the IP address for PC0:

_____

Part 5: Enable DHCP on the Other PCs

a. Click **PC1**.

b. Select **Desktop** tab.

c. Select **IP Configuration**.

d. Click **DHCP**.

Question:

Record the IP address for PC1:

_____

e. Close the configuration window.

f. Enable DHCP on **PC2**, following the steps for PC1.

Part 6: Verify Connectivity

a. Click **PC2** and select the **Desktop** tab.

b. Select **Command Prompt**.

c. Enter **ipconfig** at the prompt to view the IP configuration.

d. At the prompt, enter **ping 192.168.5.1** to ping the wireless router.

e. Enter **ping 192.168.5.126** to ping PC0 at the prompt.

f. At the prompt, enter **ping 192.168.5.127** to ping PC1.

g. The pings to all devices should be successful.

CHAPTER 12

Gateways to Other Networks

12.2.2 Packet Tracer–Examine NAT on a Wireless Router

Objectives

- Examine NAT configuration on a wireless router
- Set up four PCs to connect to a wireless router using DHCP
- Examine traffic that crosses the network using NAT

Instructions

Part 1: Examine the Configuration for Accessing External Network

a. Add one PC and connect it to the wireless router with a straight-through cable. Wait for all link lights to turn green before moving on to the next step or click **Fast Forward**.

b. On the PC, click **Desktop**. Select **IP Configuration**. Click **DHCP** to enable each device to receive an IP address via the DHCP on the wireless router.

c. Note the IP address of the default gateway. Close the **IP Configuration** when done.

d. Open a web browser and enter the IP address of the default gateway in the **URL** field. Enter the username **admin** and password **admin** when prompted.

e. Click the **Status** menu option in the upper right-hand corner. When selected, it displays the **Router** submenu page.

f. Scroll down the router page to the **Internet Connection** option. The IP address assigned here is the address assigned by the ISP. If no IP address is present (**0.0.0.0** appears), close the window, wait for a few seconds, and try again. The wireless router is in the process of obtaining an IP address from the ISP DHCP server.

The address seen here is the address assigned to the internet port on the wireless router.

Question:

Is this a private or public address?

Part 2: Examine the Configurations for Accessing the Internal Network

a. Click **Local Network** in the bold submenu bar.

b. Scroll down to examine the **Local Network** information. This is the address assigned to the internal network.

c. Scroll down further to examine the DHCP server information and range of IP addresses that can be assigned to connected hosts.

Question:

Are these private or public addresses?

_____

d. Close the wireless router configuration window.

Part 3: Connect Three PCs to the Wireless Router

a. Add three more PCs and connect them to the wireless router with straight-through cables. Wait for all link lights to turn green before moving onto the next step, or click **Fast Forward**.

b. On each PC, click **Desktop**. Select **IP Configuration**. Click **DHCP** to enable each device to receive an IP address via the DHCP on the wireless router. Close **IP Configuration** when done.

c. Click **Command Prompt** to verify each device IP configuration using the **ipconfig /all** command.

_____

Note: These devices will receive a private address. Private addresses cannot cross the internet, so, NAT translation must occur.

_____

Part 4: View NAT Translation Across the Wireless Router

a. Enter **Simulation** mode by clicking the **Simulation** tab in the lower right-hand corner next to the Realtime tab, and it is represented by a stopwatch symbol.

b. View traffic by creating a **Complex PDU** in **Simulation** mode:

1) From the **Simulation** panel, click **Show All/None** to change visible events to none. Now, click **Edit Filters,** and on the **Misc** tab, select the boxes for **TCP** and **HTTP.** Close the window when done.

2) Add a **Complex PDU** by clicking the opened envelope located in upper menu.

3) Click one of the PCs to specify it as the source.

c. Specify the Complex PDU settings by changing the following in the **Complex PDU** window:

1) Under **PDU Settings** > Select Application should be set to: **HTTP.**

2) Click ciscolearn.nat.com server to specify it as the destination device.

3) For the **Source Port,** enter **1000.**

4) Under **Simulation Settings,** select **Periodic.** Enter **120** seconds for the **Interval.**

5) Click **Create PDU** in the **Create Complex PDU** window.

d. Double-click the simulation panel to unlock it from the PT window. This allows you to move the simulation panel to view the entire network topology.

e. Observe the traffic flow by clicking **Play** in the **Simulation** panel. Speed up the animation by sliding the play control slider to the right.

Note: Click **View Previous Events** when the **Buffer Full** message is displayed.

Part 5: View the Header Information of the Packets that Traveled Across the Network

a. Examine the packet headers sent between a PC and the web server.

   1) In the **Simulation** panel, double-click the third line down in the event list. This displays an envelope in the work area representing that line.

   2) Click the envelope in the work area window to view the packet and header information.

b. Click the **Inbound PDU details** tab. Examine the packet information for the source (SRC) IP address and destination IP address.

c. Click the **Outbound PDU details** tab. Examine the packet information for the source (SRC) IP address and destination IP address.

   Notice the change in SRC IP address.

d. Click through other event lines to view those headers throughout the process.

e. When finished, click **Check Results** to check your work.

CHAPTER 13

The ARP Process

13.1.3 Packet Tracer–Identify MAC and IP Addresses

Objectives

- Part 1: Gather PDU Information for a Local Network Communication
- Part 2: Gather PDU Information for a Remote Network Communication

Background

If you are interested in a career in network administration or network security, it is important to understand normal network communication processes. In this Packet Tracer activity, you will inspect Ethernet frames and IP packets at different points in the network as they travel from source to destination. You will focus on the way that the MAC and IP addresses change depending on the destination (local or remote) and the place where the PDUs are captured.

Packet Tracer has a Simulation mode which will enable you to investigate details about how PDUs travel on networks. It enables you to check the Layer 2 MAC addressing and Layer 3 IPv4 addressing of the PDUs at different locations in the network as the PDUs flow from source to destination.

This activity is optimized for viewing PDUs as they travel on local and remote networks. You will gather PDU information in PT simulation mode and answer a series of questions about the data you collect. No device configuration is required.

Instructions

Part 1: Gather PDU Information for a Local Network Communication

In this part, you will study how a device on a local network does not need a default gateway to communicate with another device on the same local network.

Note: Review the reflection questions in Part 3 before proceeding with this part. It will give you an idea of the type of information you will need to gather.

---

a. Click host **172.16.31.3** and open the **Command Prompt**.

b. Enter the **ping 172.16.31.2** command. This command will issue a series of ICMP echo request packets to the destination. If the packets reach the destination, it will send echo-reply messages back to the source of the ping requests.

c. Click the **Simulation** mode button to switch to simulation mode. Repeat the **ping 172.16.31.2** command. An envelope icon that represents a PDU appears next to **172.16.31.3**.

d. Click the PDU and locate the following information in both the **OSI Model** and **Outbound PDU Details** tabs. The **Outbound PDU Details** tab shows simplified packet and frame headers for the PDU. You should observe the following details regarding addressing for the PDU.

- At Device: **172.16.31.3**

- Source MAC Address: **0060.7036.2849**

- Destination MAC Address: **000C:85CC:1DA7**

- Source IP Address: **172.16.31.3**

- Destination IP Address: **172.16.31.2**

e. Click **Capture / Forward (the right arrow followed by a vertical bar)**, and the PDU moves to the next step in its journey. Use the **OSI Model** tab to gather the same information from step d. Repeat this process until the PDU reaches its destination. For each step on the path to delivery, record the information for each PDU into a spreadsheet using a format like the table shown below. The information for the first step is shown in the table.

At Device	Src MAC	Dest. MAC	Src IPv4	Dest IPv4

f. You will notice that the information for the inbound PDU is unchanged.

Question:

In the **PDU Information** window, click the the **Outbound PDU** tab. How does the addressing differ, and why? Record the addressing in your table.

g. Return to **Realtime** mode.

Part 2: Gather PDU Information for a Remote Network Communication

To communicate with remote networks, a gateway device is necessary. The gateway device connects two or more networks. In this part, you will study the process that takes place when one device communicates with another device that is on a remote network. Pay close attention to the MAC addresses used.

Note: Move your mouse over the **Router.** You will see information about the addressing of the router interfaces. Refer to these addresses as you observe the PDU flow through the router.

a. Return to the **Command Prompt** for **172.16.31.3**.

b. Enter the **ping 10.10.10.2** command. The first couple of pings may time out.

c. Switch to **Simulation** mode and repeat the **ping 10.10.10.2** command. A PDU appears next to **172.16.31.3**.

d. Click the PDU and note the following information details:

- At Device: **172.16.31.3**

- Source MAC Address: **0060.7036.2849**

- Destination MAC Address: **00D0:BA8E:741A**
- Source IP Address: **172.16.31.3**
- Destination IP Address: **10.10.10.2**

Question:

What device and interface has the destination MAC address that is shown?

_____

e. Click **Capture / Forward** (the right arrow followed by a vertical bar) to move the PDU to the next device. Gather the same information from step d. Repeat this process until the PDU reaches its destination. Record the PDU information you gathered from pinging 172.16.31.5 to 10.10.10.2 into a spreadsheet using a format like the sample table shown below. Enter details for both the inbound and outbound PDUs at the router.

At Device	Src MAC	Dest. MAC	Src IPv4	Dest IPv4

f. Repeat the process for the echo-reply message that originates from host 10.10.10.2. Complete the table for each step.

At Device	Src MAC	Dest. MAC	Src IPv4	Dest IPv4

Reflection Questions

Answer the following questions regarding the captured data:

1. What different types of cables/media were used to connect devices?

_____

2. Did the cables change the handling of the PDU in any way?

_____

3. Did the wireless Access Point do anything to the PDUs that it received?

_____

4. Was PDU addressing changed by the access point?

_____

5. What was the highest OSI layer the Access Point used?

_____

6. At what OSI model layer do cables and access points operate?

_____

7. When examining the **PDU Details** tab, which MAC address appeared first, the source or the destination?

_____

8. Sometimes, PDUs were marked with red Xs while others had green checkmarks. What is the significance of these markings?

_____

9. Every time the PDU was sent between the 10 and 172 networks, the MAC addresses suddenly changed at one point. Where did that occur?

_____

10. Which device uses MAC addresses that start with 00D0:BA?

_____

11. What devices did the other MAC addresses belong to?

_____

12. Did the sending and receiving IPv4 addresses change in any of the PDUs?

_____

13. When you follow the reply to a ping, sometimes called a _pong_, what happens to the source and destination addresses?

_____

14. Why do you think the router interfaces are part of two different IP networks?

_____

15. Which IP networks are connected by the router?

_____

CHAPTER 14

Routing Between Networks

14.3.3 Packet Tracer–Observe Traffic Flow in a Routed Network

Objectives

- Part 1: Observe Traffic Flow in an Unrouted LAN
- Part 2: Reconfigure the Network to Route Between LANs
- Part 3: Observe Traffic Flow in the Routed Network

Background / Scenario

The company you work for has been asked to propose a new network design for XYZ LLC. XYZ is a startup company that has recently experienced success with their product offerings. They will be expanding, and their network will need to grow with them. Currently, the network is configured with a single IP network for hosts in all departments. This design has become inefficient, and network delays are becoming increasingly noticeable. You have been asked to help prepare the proposal with the sales team. The sales team will propose a solution in which network efficiency is enhanced by implementing routing between separate department networks. You are working on a demonstration about how having multiple routed networks in a business can improve network efficiency. Follow the instructions to help propose a new network to XYZ LLC.

Instructions

Part 1: Observe Traffic Flow in an Unrouted LAN

The XYZ network comprises about 150 devices connected to a LAN configured on a single IPv4 network. Hosts in different departments are connected to switches, which are then connected to the **Edge** router. The router only routes traffic between the LAN and the internet, represented by the **ISP** cloud. Because only one IP network is used in the LAN, all departments are on the same network.

The Packet Tracer topology is simplified. It only shows some of the departments and hosts. Assume that the behavior that you will demonstrate is happening at far greater scale than what is shown in the PT network.

In this part, you will use Packet Tracer simulation mode to observe how traffic flows through unrouted LANs.

Step 1: Clear the ARP cache on host Sales 1.

Hover your mouse over the **Sales 1** host to see its IP address. Make note of it.

a. Click **Sales 1** > the **Desktop** tab > **Command Prompt**, and then enter the **arp -a** command. There should be no MAC addresses in the ARP cache. If there are entries in the ARP cache, use the **arp -d** command to delete them.

Step 2: Observe traffic flow in the network.

    a. Click the **Simulation** mode button in the lower right-hand corner of the PT window to switch from **Realtime** to **Simulation** mode.

    b. Open the **Command Prompt** for **Sales 2**, and then enter the **ping** command followed by the **Sales 1** IP address.

    c. Use the **Capture then Forward** button (the triangle pointing to the right with a vertical bar attached) in the **Play Controls** of the **Simulation Panel** to begin executing the **ping** command. You will see a colored envelope icon appear next to **Sales 2**. This represents a PDU. Click the **Capture then Forward** button to move the PDU to the first device on its path to the destination device. Click the PDU envelope to inspect the contents.

    Questions:

    What are the source and destination MAC and IP addresses for the frame and packet?

    _____

    Why is the destination MAC address the broadcast address?

    _____

    d. Advance the PDUs through the network until a new PDU (different color) is created at **Sales 2**.

    Questions:

    Which hosts and other types of devices need to process the ARP request packets?

    _____

    What is the impact of this on the efficient operation of the network as it is currently configured?

    _____

    e. A new PDU with a different color has appeared at **Sales 2**. Click the new PDU and inspect its contents. Look at the outbound PDU details.

    Question:

    What type of PDU is this?

    _____

    f. Return to **Realtime** mode.

Part 2: Reconfigure the Network to Route Between LANs

In this part, you will demonstrate the benefits of routing between department networks. First, you will cable each network switch to connect directly to a router interface. Then, you will reconfigure the hosts to receive addresses on two new IPv4 networks that are created by the router.

Step 1: Change device connections.

The three switches are connected to each other with copper straight-through cables.

  a. For the cable that connects the **Accounting** switch with **Finance** switch, click the green triangle on the **Accounting** switch side of the link.

  b. Drag that end of the cable to the **Edge** router and connect the cable to the **GigabitEthernet 1/0** port.

  c. Repeat this step for the link between **Finance** and **Sales**. Connect to the available GigabitEthernet port.

Step 2: Configure the hosts with addresses on the new LANs.

Each interface of the **Edge** router was previously configured to put each department on its own IPv4 network. The hosts will receive their new IP addresses from the router. However, it will take time for the hosts on the **Finance** and **Sales** networks to receive their new IP addresses. (The hosts on the **Accounting** network will remain on 192.168.1.0/24.)

  a. To speed up the process of getting new IP addresses, open a **Command Prompt** on each of the four devices in the **Finance** and **Sales** networks.

  b. Enter the **ipconfig /renew** command. This will force the host to request a new IP address from the DHCP server running on the **Edge** router. You should see confirmation of new IP addressing.

    What IPv4 network is assigned to the **Finance** network?

    What IPv4 network is assigned to the **Sales** network?

Part 3: Observe Traffic Flow in the Routed Network

In this part, you will observe how traffic now flows through a routed network.

Step 1: Ping Sales 1 from Sales 2.

  a. Return to the **Command Prompt** for **Sales 2** and verify that its ARP cache is empty. If not, delete any entries.

  b. Switch to **Simulation** mode.

  c. Ping **Sales 1** from **Sales 2**.

  d. Use the **Capture then Forward** button to step the PDUs through the network. Observe how the ARP request message flows through the network this time.

    Question:

    Which devices receive the ARP broadcasts this time?

Step 2: Ping other hosts.

Repeat this demo by pinging other hosts and the internet server. Observe the flow of the ARP request PDUs.

Question:

What is the benefit of using multiple IPv4 networks, or subnetworks, within an enterprise?

_____

Note: The network topology used in the activity is for demonstration purposes only. While it is possible that a real enterprise network could use a router this way, there are more optimal topologies that achieve these results. You will learn about other design approaches in later networking courses.

14.3.4 Packet Tracer–Create a LAN

Addressing Table

Device	Interface/Port	IPv4 Address	Subnet Mask
Admin PC	NIC	DHCP	N/A
Manager PC	NIC	DHCP	N/A
Printer	NIC	192.168.1.100	255.255.255.0
www.cisco.pt	NIC	209.165.200.225	N/A

Objectives

- Connect Network Devices and Hosts

- Configure Devices with IPv4 Addressing

- Verify the End Device Configuration and Connectivity

- Use Networking Commands to View Host Information

Background / Scenario

A new branch office is opening, and you have been asked to set up the LAN. The network devices are already set up, but you need to connect them and the hosts together. You also need to configure IPv4 addressing on the end devices and verify that they can reach local and remote resources.

Instructions

Part 1: Connect Network Devices and Hosts

Step 1: Power on the end devices and Office Router.

    a. Click each device and open its **Physical** tab. **Note:** There is no power switch on the switch model used in this activity.

    b. Locate the power switch for each device in the **Physical Device View** window.

    c. Click the power switch to turn the device on. You should see a green light near the power switch to indicate that the device is powered on.

Step 2: Connect the end devices.

    Use the table and instructions to connect the network devices and hosts to create the physical network.

Connections Table

Device	Interface/Port	Connected to Device	Connection Interface/Port
Office Router	G0/0	ISP1	G0/0
Office Router	G0/1	Switch	G0/1
Admin PC	NIC (F/0)	Switch	F0/1
Manager PC	NIC (F/0)	Switch	F0/2
Printer	NIC (F/0)	Switch	F0/24

Note: In the table above, interfaces designated with **G** are GigabitEthernet interfaces. Interfaces that are designated with **F** are FastEthernet interfaces.

a. Connect the networking devices according to the information in the Connections Table using Ethernet copper straight-through cables. For the internet-to-Office Router connection, select the device and port from the dropdown menus that appear when you click the cloud with the connections tool selected.

b. Connect the two PCs and the printer to the office switch according to the information in the Connections Table. Use copper straight-through cables.

c. You should see green link lights on all connections after a brief delay.

Part 2: Configure Devices with IPv4 Addressing

Step 1: Configure the hosts with addressing information.

a. The Admin and Manager PCs should receive their IP addressing information from DHCP. The Office Router has been configured to supply IP addresses to hosts on the branch office LAN. Click the PCs and go to the **Desktop** tabs on each. Open the IP Configuration application and configure the PCs to receive their IP addresses dynamically.

b. Printers and servers are often manually configured with addressing because other devices on the network are configured to access them using IP addresses. Manual configuration with a static address will ensure that the IP addresses of these devices do not change.

1) Click the printer and open the **Config** tab.

2) Click the **FastEthernet0** interface in the left-hand pane.

3) Enter the addressing information from the Addressing Table.

c. Because the two computers are on the same network, their IPv4 addresses will be similar, and their subnet masks and default gateways will be identical.

Questions:

Why do you think the IPv4 addresses are different, but the subnet masks and default gateways are the same?

_____

The printer does not require a default gateway because it will only be accessed by hosts on the local network. However, if you need to configure it with a default gateway, which value will the printer use? How can you determine this from the other devices in the network?

_____

Part 3: Verify the End Device Configuration and Connectivity

Step 1: Verify connectivity between the two PCs.

a. Go to the PCs' desktops and check the IP addressing configuration. You should see that they have dynamically received IP addresses on the 192.168.1.0 255.255.255.0 network. You should also see that they have received addresses for the Default Gateway and DNS server settings.

    b. From the command prompt on the **Admin** PC, ping the IP address of the **Printer**. Repeat this process for the **Manager** PC. You should see successful pings for each. This verifies that the PCs and the printer are powered on, correctly connected, and addressed.

Step 2: Verify internet connectivity.

From the PCs' desktops, open a web browser. Enter the internet server's IP to display the webpage. Repeat the process, but connect using the server's URL.

Question:

If you can connect using the IP address but not via the URL, what do you think is the cause of this problem?

Part 4: Use Networking Commands to View Host Information

The networking commands available from the command prompt on PCs are very similar to those available in Windows. In this part of the activity, you will use **ipconfig** and **tracert** to learn more about the LAN.

Step 1: Use the ipconfig command.

The **ipconfig** command displays details about the addressing configured on a host.

Question:

Open a command prompt on one of the PCs, enter the **ipconfig** command, and make note of the information that is returned. Now enter the **ipconfig /all** command. What additional information is displayed?

Step 2: Use the tracert command.

The **tracert** command uses ICMP to return information about the routers that are passed as packets go from the source PC to the destination.

Trace to a remote destination by going to one of the PCs and entering **tracert**, followed by the web server's URL.

Questions:

How many routers are passed on the way to the destination? How are those routers identified?

Where is the second router located?

Reflection Question

Consider a small office that has a LAN similar to the one you have created here. What is the biggest facilities challenge when setting up the network in a new location?

CHAPTER 15

TCP and UDP

This chapter contains no labs or packet tracers.

Application Layer Services

16.1.5 Packet Tracer–The Client Interaction

Objectives

- Observe the client interaction between the server and PC.

Background / Scenario

Clients such as desktop PCs request services from servers. Using physical PCs and servers, the lab environment supports a full range of services. In a simulated environment, the number of services is limited. Packet Tracer allows the addition of simulated network servers that support DHCP, DNS, HTTP, and TFTP. Packet Tracer also supports the addition of simulated PCs that can request these services. This activity uses a simple network consisting of a PC connected directly to a server configured to supply DNS services, as well as hosting a web page through an HTTP server. This activity will track the flow of traffic that happens when a web page is requested, how the web page's IP address is resolved, and how the web page is delivered.

Instructions

Part 1: Enter Simulation Mode

When Packet Tracer starts, it presents a logical view of the network in **Realtime** mode.

Click **Simulation Mode** to enter simulation mode. The simulation mode icon is located in the bottom right-hand of the logical workplace.

Part 2: Set Event List Filters

In **Simulation** mode, the default is to capture all events. You will use filters to only capture DNS and HTTP events.

   a. In the **Event List Filters** section, click **Show All/None** to clear all the check marks.

   b. Click **Edit Filters**. On the **IPv4** tab, select **DNS**. On the **Misc** tab, select **HTTP**. Close the window when done. The **Event List Filters** shows DNS and HTTP as the only visible events.

Part 3: Request a Web Page from the PC

You will open a simulated web browser on the PC and request a web page from the server.

   a. Click **PC**. Click **Desktop** tab and click **Web Browser**.

   b. A simulated web browser opens. Type **www.example.com** into the **URL** box, click **Go** button to the right, and minimize the PC window.

Part 4: Run the Simulation

a. In the **Play Controls** section of the **Simulation Panel**, click **Play**. The exchange between the PC and the server is animated and the events are added to the **Event List**.

These events represent the PC's request to resolve the URL to an IP address, the server providing the IP address, the PC's request for the web page, the server sending the web page in two segments, and the PC's acknowledgment of the web page.

b. Click **View Previous Event** to continue when the buffer is full.

Part 5: Access a Specific PDU

a. Restore the simulated PC window. Notice there is a web page displayed in the web browser. Minimize the simulated browser window.

b. In the **Simulation Panel Event List** section, the last column contains a colored box that provides access to detailed information about an event. Click the colored box in the first row for the first event. The **PDU Information** window opens.

Part 6: Examine the Contents of the PDU Information Window

The first tab in the PDU Information window contains information about the inbound and/or outbound PDU as it relates to the OSI model. Click **Next Layer >>** repeatedly to cycle through the inbound and outbound layers and read the description in the box below the layers to get an overview of how the exchange works.

Examine the PDU information for the other events to get an overview of the entire exchange process.

16.4.3 Packet Tracer–Observe Web Request

Objectives

■ View the client/server traffic sent from a PC to a web server when requesting web services

Instructions

Part 1: Verify Connectivity to the Web Server

a. Click **External Client** and access the **Command Prompt** from the **Desktop** tab.

b. Use the **ping** command to reach the URL **ciscolearn.web.com**.

```
PC> ping ciscolearn.web.com
```

   Notice the IP address included in the ping output. This address is obtained from the DNS server and resolves to the domain name ciscolearn.web.com. All traffic forwarded across a network uses source and destination IP address information.

c. Close the **Command Prompt** window but leave the **External Client** desktop window open.

Part 2: Connect to the Web Server

a. From the **Desktop** window, access the **Web Browser.**

b. In the **URL** block, type **ciscolearn.web.com**. Be sure to read the web page that is displayed. Leave this page open.

c. Minimize the **External Client** window, but do not close it.

Part 3: View the HTML Code

a. From the logical topology, click the **ciscolearn.web.com** server.

b. Click the **Services** tab, followed by the **HTTP** tab. Next to the **index.html** file, click **(edit)**.

c. Compare the HTML markup code on the server that creates the **Web Browser** display page on the **External Client**. This may require that you re-maximize the **External Client** window if it shrunk when you opened the server window.

d. Close both the **External Client** and **web server** windows.

Part 4: Observe Traffic Between the Client and Web Server

a. Enter **Simulation** mode by clicking the **Simulation** tab in the lower-right corner.

b. Double-click the **Simulation** panel to unlock it from the PT window. This allows you to move the **Simulation** panel to view the entire network topology.

c. View traffic by creating a **Complex PDU** in **Simulation** mode.

   i. From the **Simulation** panel, select **Edit Filters.**

   ii. Click the **Misc** tab to verify that only the **TCP** and **HTTP** checkboxes are selected.

        iii. Add a **Complex PDU** by clicking the open envelope located above the **Simulation** mode icon.

        iv. Click the **External Client** to specify it as the source. The **Create Complex PDU** window will appear.

    d. Specify the **Create Complex PDU** settings by changing the following in the **Complex PDU** window:

        i. Under **PDU Settings,** Select Application should be set to **HTTP.**

        ii. Click the **ciscolearn.web.com** server to specify it as the destination device. Notice the web server's IP address will appear in the **Destination** box in the **Complex PDU** window

        iii. For the **Starting Source Port,** enter **1000.**

        iv. Under **Simulation Settings,** select **Periodic Interval** and type **120** seconds.

    e. Create the PDU by clicking the **Create PDU** box in the **Create Complex PDU** window.

        i. Observe the traffic flow by clicking **Play** in the **Simulation** panel. Speed up the animation by using the play control slider. When the **Buffer Full** window appears, click **View Previous Events** to close it.

        ii. Scroll through the **Event List.** Notice the number of packets that traveled from source to destination. HTTP is a TCP protocol that requires connection establishment and acknowledgment of receipt of packets, considerably increasing the amount of traffic overhead.

Packet Tracer
☐ **Activity**

16.5.3 Packet Tracer–Use FTP Services

Addressing Table

Device	Interface	IP Address	Subnet Mask
FTP Server (ftp.pka)	NIC	209.165.200.226	255.255.255.224

Objectives

- Upload a file to an FTP server
- Download a file from an FTP server

Background / Scenario

File Transfer Protocol (FTP) is a commonly used application to transfer files between clients and servers on the network. The server is configured to run the service where clients connect, login, and transfer files. FTP uses port 21 as the server command port to create the connection. FTP then uses port 20 for data transfer.

In this activity, you will upload a file to an FTP server. You will also download a file from an FTP server.

Instructions

Part 1: Upload a File to an FTP Server

In this part, you will locate the **sampleFile.txt** file and upload it to an FTP server.

Step 1: Locate the file.

    a. Click **PC-A.**

    b. Click **Desktop.**

    c. Click **Command Prompt.**

    d. At the prompt, click **?** to list the available commands.

    e. Enter **dir** to see the files on the PC. Notice that there is a **sampleFile.txt** file in the C:\ directory.

```
C:\> dir
Volume in drive C has no label.
Volume Serial Number is 5E12-4AF3
Directory of C:\
12/31/1969 17:0 PM 26 sampleFile.txt
26 bytes 1 File(s)
```

Step 2: Connect to the FTP server.

    a. FTP to the FTP server at **209.165.200.226** or **ftp.pka.**

```
C:\> ftp 209.165.200.226
Trying to connect...209.165.200.226
Connected to 209.165.200.226
```

    b. Enter the username **student** and password **class** to gain access.

```
220- Welcome to PT Ftp server
Username:student
331- Username ok, need password
Password:
230- Logged in
(passive mode On)
```

Step 3: Upload a file to an FTP server.

    a. Enter **?** to see the commands available in the FTP client.

```
ftp> ?
            ?
            cd
            delete
            dir
            get
            help
            passive
            put
            pwd
            quit
            rename
ftp>
```

    b. Enter **dir** to see the files available on the server.

```
ftp> dir
Listing /ftp directory from 192.168.1.3:
0 : asa842-k8.bin 5571584
1 : asa923-k8.bin 30468096
2 : c1841-advipservicesk9-mz.124-15.T1.bin 33591768
3 : c1841-ipbase-mz.123-14.T7.bin 13832032
<output omitted>
```

    c. Enter **put sampleFile.txt** to send the file to the server.

```
ftp> put sampleFile.txt
Writing file sampleFile.txt to 209.165.200.226:
File transfer in progress...
[Transfer complete - 26 bytes]
26 bytes copied in 0.08 secs (325 bytes/sec)
ftp>
```

    d. Use the **dir** command again to list the contents of the FTP server to verify that the file has been uploaded.

Part 2: Download a File from an FTP Server

You can also download a file from an FTP server. In this part, you will rename the file **sampleFile.txt** and download it from the FTP server.

Step 1: Rename the file on an FTP server.

a. At the **ftp>** prompt, rename the **sampleFile.txt** to **sampleFile_FTP.txt** file.

```
ftp> rename sampleFile.txt sampleFile_FTP.txt
Renaming sampleFile.txt
ftp>
[OK Renamed file successfully from sampleFile.txt to sampleFile_FTP.txt]
ftp>
```

b. At the **ftp>** prompt, enter **dir** to verify the file has been renamed.

Step 2: Download the file from the FTP server.

a. Enter the command **get sampleFile_FTP.txt** to retrieve the file from the server.

```
ftp> get sampleFile_FTP.txt
Reading file sampleFile_FTP.txt from 209.165.200.226:
File transfer in progress...
[Transfer complete - 26 bytes]
26 bytes copied in 0.013 secs (2000 bytes/sec)
ftp>
```

b. Enter **quit** to exit the FTP client.

c. Display the contents of the directory on the PC again to see the image file from the FTP server.

Step 3: Delete the file from the FTP server.

a. Log in to the FTP server again to delete the **sampleFile_FTP.txt** file.

b. Enter the command to delete the **sampleFile_FTP.txt** file from the server.

Question:

What command did you use to remove the file from the FTP server?

_____

c. Enter **quit** to exit the FTP client.

Packet Tracer
☐ Activity

16.6.4 Packet Tracer–Use Telnet and SSH

Addressing Table

Device	Interface	IP Address	Subnet Mask
HQ	G0/0/1	64.100.1.1	255.255.255.0
PC0	NIC	DHCP	
PC1	NIC	DHCP	

Objectives

In this activity, you will establish a remote connection to a router using Telnet and SSH.

- Verify connectivity
- Access a remote device

Instructions

Part 1: Verify Connectivity

In this part, you will verify that the PC has IP addressing and can ping the remote router.

Step 1: Verify IP address on a PC.

   a.   From a PC, click **Desktop**. Click **Command Prompt**.

   b.   At the prompt, verify that the PC has an IP address from DHCP.

   Question:

   What command did you use to verify the IP address from DHCP?

_____

Step 2: Verify connectivity to HQ.

   Verify that you can ping the router **HQ** using the IP address listed in the **Addressing Table**.

Part 2: Access a Remote Device

In this part, you will attempt to establish a remote connection using Telnet and SSH.

Step 1: Telnet to HQ.

   At the prompt, enter the **telnet 64.100.1.1** command.

   Question:

   Were you successful? What was the output?

_____

Step 2: SSH to HQ.

The router is properly configured to not allow insecure Telnet access. You must use SSH. At the prompt, enter the **ssh -l admin 64.100.1.1** command. Enter the **class** password when prompted.

```
C:\> ssh -l admin 64.100.1.1
Password:
```

Question:

What is prompt after accessing the router successfully via SSH?

CHAPTER 17

Network Testing Utilities

Packet Tracer ☐ Activity

17.1.3 Packet Tracer–Use the ipconfig Command

Objectives

- Use the **ipconfig** command to identify incorrect configuration on a PC

Background / Scenario

A small business owner cannot connect to the internet with one of the four PCs in the office. All the PCs are configured with static IP addressing using the 192.168.1.0 /24 network. The PCs should be able to access the **www.cisco.pka** webserver. Use the **ipconfig /all** command to identify which PC is incorrectly configured.

Instructions

Part 1: Verify Configurations

a. Access the **Command Prompt** on each PC, and type the command **ipconfig /all** at the prompt.

b. Examine the IP address, subnet mask, and default gateway configuration for each PC. Be sure to record this IP configuration for each PC to help identify any PCs that are incorrectly configured.

Part 2: Correct Any Misconfigurations

a. Select the PC that is incorrectly configured.

b. Choose IP Configuration on the Desktop tab to correct the misconfiguration.

17.1.6 Packet Tracer–Use the ping Command

Objectives

- Use the **ping** command to identify an incorrect configuration on a PC.

Background / Scenario

A small business owner learns that some users are unable to access a website. All PCs are configured with static IP addressing. Use the **ping** command to identify the issue.

Instructions

Part 1: Verify Connectivity

Open the **Desktop** tab and choose **Web Browser** for each PC and enter the URL **www.cisco. pka**. Identify any PCs that are not connecting to the web server.

Note: All the devices require time to complete the boot process. Please allow up to one minute before receiving a web response.

Question:

Which PCs are unable to connect to the web server?

Part 2: Ping the Web Server from a PC with Connectivity Issues

a. On the PC, access the **Command Prompt** from the **Desktop** tab.

b. At the prompt, enter **ping www.cisco.pka.**

Question:

Did the ping return a reply? What IP address is displayed in the reply, if any?

Part 3: Ping the Web Server from Correctly Configured PCs

a. On the PC, access the **Command Prompt** from the **Desktop** tab.

b. At the prompt, enter **ping www.cisco.pka.**

Question:

Did the **ping** return a reply? What IP address is returned, if any?

Part 4: Ping the IP address of the Web Server from PCs with Connectivity Issues

a. On the PC, access the **Command Prompt** from the **Desktop** tab.

b. Attempt to reach the IP address of the web server with the **ping** command.

Question:

Did the **ping** return a reply? If so, then the PC can reach the web server via IP address, but not domain name. This could indicate a problem with the DNS server configuration on the PC.

Part 5: Compare the DNS Server Information on the PCs

a. Access the **Command Prompt** of the PCs without any issues.

b. Using the command **ipconfig /all**, examine the DNS server configuration on the PCs without any issues.

c. Access the **Command Prompt** of the PCs with connectivity issues.

d. Using the command **ipconfig /all**, examine the DNS server configuration on the PCs with misconfigurations. Do the two configurations match?

Part 6: Make Any Necessary Configuration Changes on the PCs

a. Navigate to the **Desktop** tab on the PCs with issues and make any necessary configuration changes in **IP Configuration**.

b. Use connect to **www.cisco.pka** to verify that the configuration changes resolved the problem.

18.2.3 Lab–View Wireless and Wired NIC Information

Objectives

- Part 1: Identify and Work with PC NICs
- Part 2: Identify and Use the System Tray Network Icons

Background / Scenario

This lab requires you to determine the availability and status of the network interface cards (NICs) on the PC. Windows provides a number of ways to view and work with your NICs.

In this lab, you will access the NIC information of the PC and change the status of these cards.

Required Resources

- One PC (Windows 10 with two NICs—wired and wireless—and a wireless connection)
- A wireless router

Instructions

Part 1: Identify and Work with PC NICs

In Part 1, you will identify the NIC types on the PC. You will explore different ways to extract information about these NICs and how to activate and deactivate them.

Note: This lab was performed using a PC running the Windows 10 operating system. You should be able to perform the lab with another Windows operating systems version. However, menu selections and screens may vary.

Step 1: Use network connections.

You will verify which network connections are available.

a. Right-click **Start** and select **Network Connections**.

b. The **Network Connections** window displays the list of NICs available on this PC. Look for your **Local Area Connection** and **Wireless Network Connection** adapters in this window.

Note: If the **Network status** page is displayed, click **Change adapter options** to navigate to the **Network Connections** window.

Note: Other types of network adapters, such as **Bluetooth Network connection** and **Virtual Private Network (VPN) adapter**, may also be displayed in this window.

Step 2: Work with your wireless NIC.

Verify the wireless network connection settings.

a.   Select the Wireless Network Connection option. Right-click on it to display a drop-down list. The first option displays if your wireless NIC is enabled or disabled. If your wireless NIC is disabled, you will have an option to **Enable** it.

b.   Verify that the wireless network is connected. If not, click **Connect/Disconnect** to connect to the desired network. Click **Status** to open the **Wireless Network Connection Status** window.

Questions:

What is the Service Set Identifier (SSID) for the wireless router of your connection?

_____

What is the speed of your wireless connection?

_____

c.   Click **Details** to display the **Network Connection Details** window.

Question:

What is the MAC address of your wireless NIC?

_____

d.   Open a command prompt and enter **ipconfig /all**.

```
C:\Users\Bob> ipconfig /all
```

Notice the information displayed is similar to the **Network Connection Details** window information. When you have reviewed the details, click **Close** to return to the **Wireless Network Connection Status** window.

e.   Return to the **Wireless Network Connection Status** window. Click **Wireless Properties** to open the Home-Net network's **Wireless Network Properties** window.

f.   You should always use wireless security whenever available. To verify (or configure) the wireless security options, click on the **Security** tab.

The window displays the type of security and encryption method enabled. You can also enter (or change) the security key in this window. Close all windows.

Step 3: Work with your wired NIC.

We will now verify the wired network connection settings.

a.   Open the **Network Connections** window by right-clicking Windows **Start** and choosing **Network Connections**.

_____

Note: If the **Network status** page is displayed, click **Change adapter options** to navigate to the **Network Connections** window.

_____

b.   Right-click the **Local Area Connection** option to display the drop-down list. If the NIC is disabled, enable it.

c.   Click the **Status** option to open the **Local Area Connection Status** window. This window displays information about your wired connection to the LAN.

   d. Click **Details** to view the address information for your LAN connection.

   e. Open a command prompt and enter **ipconfig /all**. Find your **Local Area Connection** information and compare it with the information displayed in the Network Connection Details window.

   f. Close all windows on your desktop.

Part 2: Identify and Use the System Tray Network Icons

In Part 2, you will use the network icons in your system tray to display the networks available on the network.

   a. The bottom right-hand corner of the Windows 10 screen contains the system tray. Move your mouse to display the system tray.

   b. If you hover over the network icon in the system tray, it displays the currently connected networks.

   c. Click the wireless network icon, and it displays the wired and wireless network SSIDs that are in range of your wireless NIC.

   d. Right-click the wireless network icon, and it displays a troubleshooting option and an option to open the Network and Sharing Center window.

   e. Click the **Open Network and Sharing Center** option.

   f. The **Network and Sharing Center** is a central window that displays information about the active network or networks, the network type, the type of access.

Reflection Question

Why would you activate more than one NIC on a PC?

CHAPTER 19

Cloud and Virtualization

19.2.3 Lab–Install Linux in a Virtual Machine and Explore the GUI

Objectives

- Part 1: Prepare a Computer for Virtualization
- Part 2: Install a Linux OS on the Virtual Machine
- Part 3: Explore the GUI

Background / Scenario

Computing power and resources have increased tremendously over the last 10 years. A benefit of multi-core processors and large amounts of RAM is the ability to install multiple operating systems through the use of virtualization on a computer.

With virtualization, one or more virtual computers can operate inside one physical computer. Virtual computers running within physical computers are called *virtual machines*. Virtual machines are often called *guests*, and physical computers are often called *hosts*. Anyone with a modern computer and operating system can run virtual machines.

In this lab, you will install a Linux OS in a virtual machine using a desktop virtualization application, such as VirtualBox. After completing the installation, you will explore the GUI interface. You will also explore the command-line interface using this virtual machine in a lab later in this course.

Required Resources

- Computer with a minimum of 2 GB of RAM and 10 GB of free disk space
- High-speed internet access to download Oracle VirtualBox and a Linux OS image, such as Ubuntu Desktop

Instructions

Part 1: Prepare a Computer for Virtualization

In Part 1, you will download and install desktop virtualization software and a Linux OS image. Your instructor may provide you with a Linux OS image.

Step 1: Download and install VirtualBox.

VMware Player and Oracle VirtualBox are two virtualization programs that you can download and install to support the OS image file. In this lab, you will use the VirtualBox application.

a. Navigate to **https://www.virtualbox.org/**. Click the download link on this page.

b. Choose and download the appropriate installation file based on your operating system.

c. After the VirtualBox installation file is downloaded, run the installer and accept the default installation settings.

Step 2: Download a Linux image.

a. Navigate to the Ubuntu website at **http://www.ubuntu.com**. Click the **Download** link on this page to download and save an Ubuntu Desktop image.

Step 3: Create a new virtual machine.

a. Click **Start** and search for **Virtualbox**. Click **Oracle VM VirtualBox** to open the manager. When the manager opens, click **New** to start the Ubuntu installation.

b. On the **Name and operating system** screen, type **Ubuntu** in the **Name** field. In the **Type** field, select **Linux**. In the **Version** field, select the corresponding downloaded version. Click **Next** to continue.

c. On the **Memory size** screen, increase the amount of RAM if the amount of RAM for the virtual machine is in the green area. Going beyond the green area would adversely affect the performance of the host. Click **Next** to continue.

d. On the **Hard disk** screen, click **Create** to create a virtual hard disk.

e. On the **Hard disk file type** screen, use the default **VDI (VirtualBox Disk Image)** file type settings. Click **Next** to continue.

f. On the **Storage on physical hard disk** screen, use the default **dynamically allocated** storage settings. Click **Next** to continue.

g. On the **File location and size** screen, you can adjust the hard drive and change the name and location of the virtual hard drive. Click **Create** to use the default settings.

h. When the hard drive creation is done, the new virtual machine is listed in the **Oracle VM VirtualBox Manager** window. Select **Ubuntu** and click **Start** in the top menu.

Part 2: Install Ubuntu on the Virtual Machine

Step 1: Mount the image.

a. In the **Oracle VM Virtualbox Manager** window, right-click **Ubuntu** and select **Settings**. In the **Ubuntu – Settings** window, click **Storage** in the left pane and **Empty** in the middle pane. In the right pane, click the CD symbol and select the file location of the Ubuntu image. Click **OK** to continue.

b. In the **Oracle VM VirtualBox Manager** window, click **Start** in the top menu.

Figure 19-1   Ubuntu - Settings

Step 2: Install the OS.

a. On the **Welcome** screen, you are prompted to try or install Ubuntu. The try option does not install the OS; it runs the OS straight from the image. In this lab, you will install the Ubuntu OS on this virtual machine. Click **Install Ubuntu**.

b. Follow the on-screen instructions and provide the necessary information when prompted.

Note: If you are not connected to the internet, you can continue to install and enable the network later.

---

c. Because this Ubuntu installation is on a virtual machine, it is safe to erase the disk and install Ubuntu without affecting the host computer. Select **Erase disk and install Ubuntu**. Otherwise, installing Ubuntu on a physical computer will erase all data on the disk and replace the existing operating system with Ubuntu. Click **Install Now** to start the installation.

d. Click **Continue** to erase the disk and install Ubuntu.

e. On the **Who are you?** screen, provide your name and choose a password. You can use the generated username or enter a different username. Choose a password. If desired, you can change the other settings. Click **Continue**.

f. The Ubuntu OS is now installing on the virtual machine. This will take several minutes. When the **Installation is complete** message displays, return to the **Oracle VM Virtualbox Manager** window. Right-click **Ubuntu** and select **Settings**. In the **Ubuntu – Settings** window, click **Storage** in the left pane. Click the mounted Ubuntu image in the middle pane. In the right pane, click the CD symbol and click **Remove Disk from Virtual Drive**. Click **OK** to continue.

g. On the Ubuntu VM, click **Restart Now**.

Part 3: Explore the GUI

In this part, you will install the VirtualBox guest additions and explore the Ubuntu GUI.

Step 1: Install Guest Additions.

a. Log in to your Ubuntu virtual machine using the user credentials created in the previous part.

b. Your Ubuntu Desktop window may be smaller than expected. This is especially true on high-resolution displays. Click **Device > Insert Guest Additions CD image...** to install the Guest Additions, which allows more functions, such as changing the virtual machine's screen resolution.

Figure 19-2   Ubuntu - Oracle VM VirtualBox

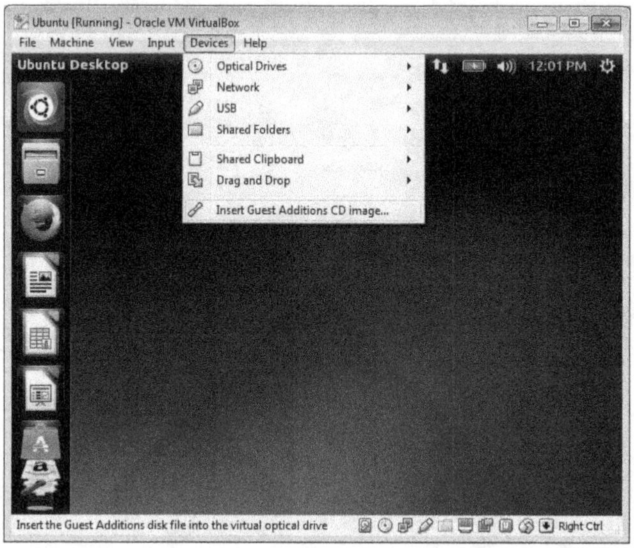

c. Click **Run** to install the additions. When prompted for a password, use the same password that you used to log on. Click **Authenticate** to continue.

d. If the computer was not connected to the internet during the installation, choose **Devices > Network Settings** from the Oracle VirtualBox menu. Enable network adapters and configure the proper settings for network connections as necessary. Click **OK**.

e. the installation of the additions is done, restart the virtual machine again. Click the menu in the upper-right corner and click **Shut down**. Click **Restart** to restart Ubuntu.

Step 2: Open a web browser.

a. Log in to Ubuntu again to resize the virtual machine window.

b. Open a web browser. Depending on the Linux distribution, you can use the web browser link installed on the desktop; if no browser was installed, you might need to search for one.

c. Locate a terminal emulator to access the command-line interface. You will be using a terminal emulator in later labs.

d. Explore the installed Linux distribution and locate a few applications that you can use.

Reflection Question

What are the advantages and disadvantages of using a virtual machine?

CHAPTER 20

Number Systems

This chapter contains no labs or packet tracers.

21.1.4 Lab–Determine the MAC Address of a Host

Addressing Table

Device	Interface	IP Address	Subnet Mask
PC	VLAN 1	192.168.1.2	255.255.255.0

Objectives

- Determine the MAC address of a Windows computer on an Ethernet network using the ipconfig /all command
- Analyze a MAC address to determine the manufacturer

Background / Scenario

Every computer on an Ethernet local network has a Media Access Control (MAC) address burned into the Network Interface Card (NIC). Computer MAC addresses are usually displayed as six sets of two hexadecimal numbers separated by dashes or colons (example: 15-EF-A3-45-9B-57). The ipconfig /all command displays the computer MAC address. You may work individually or in teams.

Required Resources

- PC running Windows 10 with at least one Ethernet network interface card (NIC)
- Connectivity to the internet

Instructions

Part 1: Locating the MAC Address on a Computer

In this part of the lab, you will determine the MAC address of a computer using the Windows ipconfig command.

Step 1: Display information for the command *ipconfig / all*.

    a. Right-click the Start button and select **Command Prompt**.

    b. Enter the ipconfig /all command at the command prompt.

Step 2: Locate the MAC (physical) address(es) in the output from the *ipconfig /all* command.

Use the table below to fill in the description of the Ethernet adapter and the Physical (MAC) Address:

Description	Physical Address

Question:

How many MAC addresses did you discover in your PC?

Part 2: Analyzing the Parts of a MAC Address

Every Ethernet network interface has a physical address assigned to it when it is manufactured. These addresses are 48-bits (6 bytes) long and are written in hexadecimal notation. MAC addresses are made up of two parts. One part of the MAC address—the first 3 bytes—represents the vendor that manufactured the network interface. This part of the MAC is called the OUI (Organizationally Unique Identifier). Each vendor that wants to make and sell Ethernet network interfaces must register with the IEEE in order to be assigned an OUI.

The second part of the address—the remaining 3 bytes—are the unique ID for the interface. All MAC addresses beginning with the same OUI must have unique values in the last 3 bytes.

In this example, the physical MAC address for the Ethernet LAN interface is D4-BE-D9-13-63-00.

Manufacturer OUI	Unique Identifier for the Interface	Vendor Name
D4-BE-D9	13-63-00	Dell Incorporated

Step 1: List MAC addresses discovered by you and your classmates in the previous part.

List the 3-byte Manufacturer OUI, the 3-byte unique interface identifier and the vendor name in the table below.

Manufacturer OUI	Unique Identifier for the Interface	Vendor Name

Step 2: Look up the vendors who are the registered owners of the OUI you listed in the table.

a. Wireshark.org provides an easy-to-use lookup tool at **https://www.wireshark. org/tools/oui-lookup.html**. Use this tool or use the internet to search for other ways to identify an OUI.

b. Use the information you found to update the vendor column in the chart in Step 1.

Question:

How many different vendors did you discover?

Reflection Questions

1. Why might a computer have more than one MAC address?

2. The sample output from the **ipconfig /all** command shown previously had only one MAC address. Suppose the output was from a computer that also had wireless Ethernet capability. How might the output change?

_____

3. Try connecting and disconnecting the network cable(s) to your network adapter(s) and use the **ipconfig /all** command, again. What changes do you see? Does the MAC address still display? Will the MAC address ever change?

_____

4. What are other names for the MAC address?

_____

21.2.6 Lab–Install Wireshark

Objectives

In this activity, you will download and install Wireshark and capture packets.

- Part 1: Download Wireshark
- Part 2: Install Wireshark
- Part 3: Capture Packets Using Wireshark

Background / Scenario

Wireshark is a software protocol analyzer, or "packet sniffer" application, used for network troubleshooting, analysis, software and protocol development, and education. As data streams travel back and forth over the network, the sniffer "captures" each protocol data unit (PDU). It can then decode and analyze the content of the PDU according to the appropriate RFC or other specifications.

Wireshark is a useful tool for anyone working with networks and can be used with many labs in networking courses for data analysis and troubleshooting. This lab provides instructions for downloading and installing Wireshark.

Required Resources

- One PC with operating system of your choice that can support Wireshark
- Internet access

Instructions

Wireshark has become the industry-standard packet-sniffer program used by network engineers. This open-source software is available for many different operating systems, including Windows, Mac, and Linux. In this lab, you will download and install the Wireshark software program on your PC.

Note: Before downloading Wireshark, check with your instructor about your school's software download policy.

Part 1: Download Wireshark

a. Download Wireshark from **www.wireshark.org**.

Note: If you are using a Linux distribution, skip to the next part.

b. Choose the software version based on your PC's architecture and operating system.

c. After making a selection, the download should start. The location of the downloaded file depends on your browser and operating system.

Part 2: Install Wireshark

In this part, Wireshark installation instructions for Windows, iOS, and Ubuntu operating systems are provided for your reference. The installation procedure can vary depending on your operating system version.

Step 1: Install Wireshark on Windows.

a. The downloaded file is named **Wireshark-win64-x.x.x.exe**, where **x** represents the version number if you downloaded the 64-bit version. Double-click the file to start the installation process.

   Respond to any security messages that may display on your screen. If you already have a copy of Wireshark on your PC, you will be prompted to uninstall the old version before installing the new one. It is recommended that you remove the old version of Wireshark prior to installing a new version. Click **Yes** to uninstall the previous version of Wireshark.

b. Navigate to the Wireshark Setup wizard if this is your first time installing Wireshark, or do so after completing the uninstallation. Click **Next**.

c. Continue advancing through the installation process. Click **I Agree** when the **License Agreement** window displays.

d. Keep the default settings in the **Choose Components** window and click **Next**.

e. Choose your desired shortcut options and click **Next**.

f. You can change Wireshark's installation location, but unless you have limited disk space, it is recommended that you keep the default location. Click **Next** to continue.

g. To capture live network data, Npcap must be installed on your PC. If Npcap is already installed on your PC, the **Install** check box will be unchecked. If your installed version of Npcap is older than the version that comes with Wireshark, it is recommended that you allow the newer version to be installed by clicking the **Install Npcap x.x.x** (version number) checkbox. Click **Next** to continue.

h. **Do NOT** install USBPcap for normal traffic capture. **Do NOT select the install USBPcap** checkbox. USBPcap is experimental, and it could cause USB problems on your PC. Click **Install** to continue.

i. Wireshark starts installing its files and displays the installation status.

j. If you are installing Npcap, accept the license agreement in the Npcap Setup Wizard. Click **I Agree** to continue. Click **Install** to install Npcap. Click **Next** to finish the Npcap installation, and click **Finish** to exit the Npcap installation.

k. Click **Next** when the Wireshark installation is complete.

l. Click **Finish** to complete the Wireshark install process. Reboot the computer if necessary.

Step 2: Install Wireshark on MAC.

a. Locate and open the downloaded file.

   The downloaded file is in the form of Wireskark.x.x.x.Arm 64.dmg or Wireshark x.x.x Intel 64 .img, where x.x.x is the Wireshark version. Locate and open the downloaded file.

b. Before you begin the installation, it is a good idea to review the **Read me first.html** file.

c. To install Wireshark, drag the **Wireshark** application bundle to the Application folder to copy it there.

d. For **Wireshark** to capture packets, double-click **Install ChmodBFP.pkg.**to start the installation wizard. Follow the wizard's instructions and use the default settings unless you desire customized settings. Provide your password when prompted.

Step 3: Install Wireshark on Ubuntu Linux.

Wireshark is available from the repository for major Linux distributions. The following instructions mainly focus on the Ubuntu distribution.

a. Install Wireshark from the repository. Provide your password and enter **y** to continue the installation.

```
user@Ubuntu:~$ sudo apt-get install wireshark
[sudo] password for user:
Reading package lists... Done
Building dependency tree
Reading state information... Done
The following additional packages will be installed:
Need to get 32.9 MB of archives.
After this operation, 163 MB of additional disk space will be used.
Do you want to continue? [Y/n] y
```

b. You will be prompted to give permission to allow non-superusers to capture packets. Review the information. Use the arrows to highlight **<Yes>** if you choose to allow non-superusers to capture packets.

c. Add the current user to the wireshark group.

```
user@Ubuntu:~$ sudo usermod -aG wireshark $(whoami)
```

Note: If you need to change your reply, enter the following command at the terminal.

```
user@Ubuntu:~$ sudo dpkg-reconfigure wireshark-common
```

d. Allow the wireshark group to access the /usr/bin/dumpcap file.

```
user@Ubuntu:~$ sudo chmod +x /usr/bin/dumpcap
```

e. Log out and log back in or reboot for the changes to take effect.

Part 3: Capture Packets Using Wireshark

Now that you have successfully installed Wireshark, let's capture a few packets on your network.

a. Start Wireshark.

b. You should see a list of network interfaces you can use to capture traffic. Double-click the desired network device interface with network traffic to start the capture.

If successful, you should see packets populate the main Wireshark screen. Trouble-shoot as necessary and refer to documentation at **www.wireshark.org** for more information.

21.2.7 Lab–Use Wireshark to Examine Ethernet Frames

Objectives

- Part 1: Examine the Header Fields in an Ethernet II Frame
- Part 2: Use Wireshark to Capture and Analyze Ethernet Frames

Background / Scenario

When upper-layer protocols communicate with each other, data flows down the Open Systems Interconnection (OSI) layers and is encapsulated in a Layer-2 frame. The frame composition is dependent up on the media access type. For example, if the upper-layer protocols are TCP and IP and the media access is Ethernet, then the Layer-2 frame encapsulation will be Ethernet II (Typical for a LAN environment.)

When learning about Layer-2 concepts, it is helpful to analyze frame header information. In Part 1, you will review the fields contained in an Ethernet II frame. In Part 2, you will use Wireshark to capture and analyze Ethernet II frame header fields for local and remote traffic.

Required Resources

- One PC (your choice of operating system with Wireshark installed)
- Internet access

Instructions

Part 1: Examine the Header Fields in an Ethernet II Frame

In this part, you will examine the header fields and content in an Ethernet II frame. A Wireshark capture will be used to examine the contents in those fields.

Step 1: Review the Ethernet II header field descriptions and lengths.

Preamble	Destination Address	Source Address	Frame Type	Data	FCS
8 Bytes	6 Bytes	6 Bytes	2 Bytes	46 – 1500 Bytes	4 Bytes

Step 2: Examine the network configuration of the PC.

In this example, this PC host IP address is 192.168.1.147, and the default gateway has an IP address of 192.168.1.1. (For Linux and MAC OS, use the **ifconfig** command in the terminal.)

```
C:\> ipconfig /all
Ethernet adapter Ethernet:
    Connection-specific DNS Suffix  . :
    Description . . . . . . . . . . . : Intel(R) 82579LM Gigabit Network
Connection
    Physical Address. . . . . . . . . : F0-1F-AF-50-FD-C8
    DHCP Enabled. . . . . . . . . . . : Yes
    Autoconfiguration Enabled . . . . : Yes
```

```
        Link-local IPv6 Address . . . . . . : fe80::58c5:45f2:7e5e:29c2%11
(Preferred)
        IPv4 Address. . . . . . . . . . . : 192.168.1.147(Preferred)
        Subnet Mask . . . . . . . . . . . : 255.255.255.0
        Lease Obtained. . . . . . . . . . : Friday, September 6, 2019 11:08:36 AM
        Lease Expires . . . . . . . . . . : Saturday, September 7, 2019 11:08:36 AM
        Default Gateway . . . . . . . . . : 192.168.1.1
        DHCP Server . . . . . . . . . . . : 192.168.1.1
<output omitted>
```

Step 3: Examine Ethernet frames in a Wireshark capture.

The screenshots of the Wireshark capture below show the packets generated by a ping being issued from a PC host to its default gateway. A filter (arp or icmp) has been applied to Wireshark to view the ARP (address resolution protocol) and ICMP protocols only. ARP is a communication protocol used for determining the MAC address that is associated with the IP address. The session begins with an ARP query and reply for the gateway router's MAC address, followed by four ping requests and replies.

This screenshot highlights an ARP request's frame details.

Figure 21-1a   Ethernet

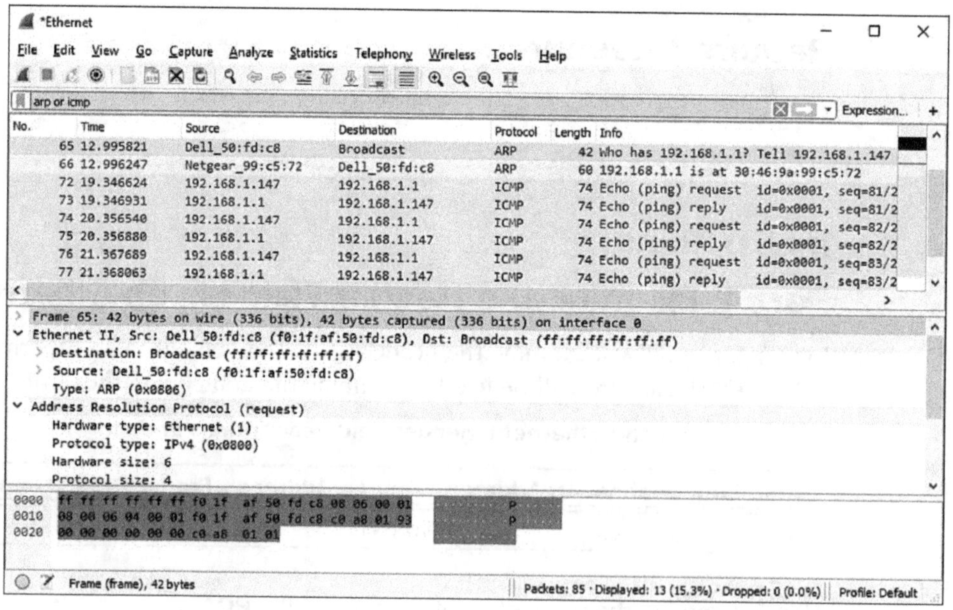

This screenshot highlights the ARP reply's frame details.

Figure 21-1b Ethernet

Step 4: Examine the Ethernet II header contents of an ARP request.

The following table takes the first frame in the Wireshark capture and displays the data in the Ethernet II header fields.

Field	Value	Description
Preamble	Not shown in capture	This field contains synchronizing bits processed by the NIC (network interface card).
Destination Address	Broadcast (ff:ff:ff:ff:ff:ff)	This field contains Layer-2 addresses for the frame. Each address is 48 bits long—or 6 octets—expressed as 12 hexadecimal digits: 0-9,A-F. A common format is 12:34:56:78:9A:BC. The first six hex numbers indicate the manufacturer of the NIC; the last six hex numbers are the NIC's serial number.
Source Address	Netgear_99:c5:72 (30:46:9a:99:c5:72)	The destination address may be a broadcast, which contains all ones, or a unicast. The source address is always unicast.
Frame Type	0x0806	For Ethernet II frames, this field contains a hexadecimal value used to indicate the type of upper-layer protocol in the data field. There are numerous upper-layer protocols supported by Ethernet II. Two common frame types are: Value　　　Description 0x0800　　IPv4 Protocol 0x0806　　Address Resolution Protocol (ARP)
Data	ARP	Contains the encapsulated upper-level protocol. The data field is between 46 – 1,500 bytes.
FCS	Not shown in capture	Frame Check Sequence is used by the NIC to identify errors during transmission. The value is computed by the sending device, encompassing frame addresses, type, and data field. It is verified by the receiver.

Questions:

What is significant about the contents of the destination address field?

_____

Why does the PC send out a broadcast ARP prior to sending the first ping request?

_____

What is the MAC address of the source in the first frame?

_____

What is the Vendor ID (OUI) of the Source NIC in the ARP request?

_____

What portion of the MAC address is the OUI?

_____

What is the NIC serial number of the source?

_____

Part 2: Use Wireshark to Capture and Analyze Ethernet Frames

In this part, you will use Wireshark to capture local and remote Ethernet frames. You will then examine the information contained in the frame header fields.

Step 1: Determine the IP address of the default gateway on your PC.

Open a command prompt window and issue the **ipconfig** command. (For Linux and MAC OS, enter the command **netstat -rn** at a terminal.)

Question:

Record the IP address of the PC default gateway?

_____

Step 2: Start capturing traffic on your PC NIC.

a. Open Wireshark to start the data capture. Double-click the desired network device interface with network traffic to start the capture.

b. Observe the traffic that appears in the packet list window.

Step 3: Filter Wireshark to display only ICMP traffic.

You can use the filter in Wireshark to block visibility of unwanted traffic. The filter does not block the capture of unwanted data; it only filters what you want to display on the screen. For now, only ICMP traffic will be displayed.

In the Wireshark **Filter** box, type **icmp**. The box should turn green if you typed the filter correctly. If the box is green, click **Apply** (the right arrow) to apply the filter.

Step 4: From the command-prompt window, ping your PC's default gateway.

From the command-prompt window, ping the default gateway using the IP address you recorded in Step 1.

Step 5: Stop capturing traffic on the NIC.

Click the **Stop Capturing Packets** icon (the red square) to stop capturing traffic.

Step 6: Examine the first Echo (ping) request in Wireshark.

The Wireshark main window is divided into three sections: the **Packet List** pane (top), the **Packet Details** pane (middle), and the **Packet Bytes** pane (bottom). If you previously selected the correct interface for packet capturing, Wireshark should display the ICMP information in Wireshark's packet list pane PC NIC's.

Figure 21-1c   Ethernet

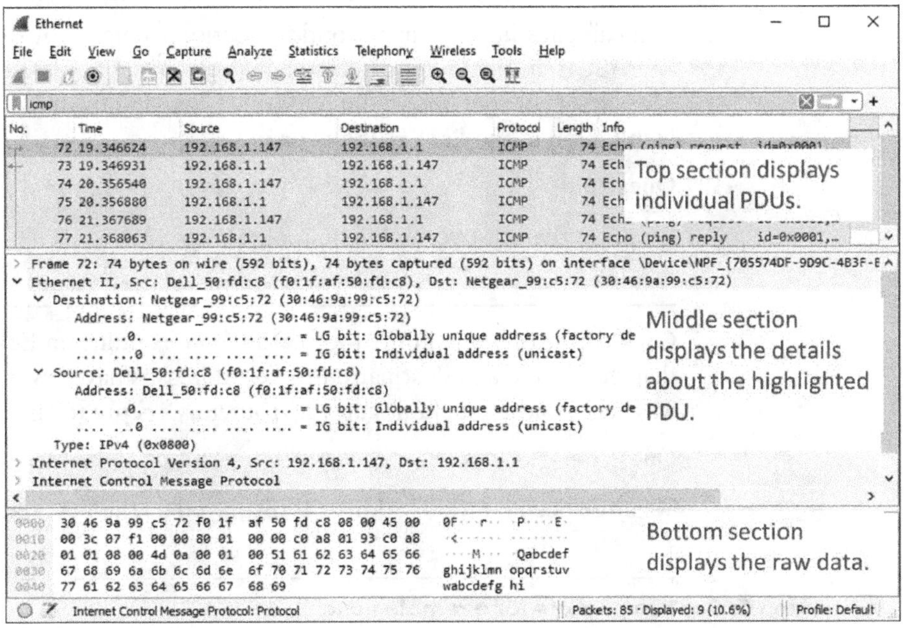

a. In the packet list pane (top section), click the first frame listed. You should see **Echo (ping) request** under the **Info** heading. The line should now be highlighted.

b. Examine the first line in the packet details pane (middle section). This line displays the length of the frame.

c. The second line in the packet details pane shows that it is an Ethernet II frame. The source and destination MAC addresses are also displayed.

Questions:

What is the MAC address PC's?

_____

What is the default gateway's MAC address?

_____

d. Click the (>) character at the beginning of the second line to obtain more information about the Ethernet II frame.

Question:

What type of frame is displayed?

_____

e. The last two lines displayed in the middle section provide information about the frame's data field. Notice that the data contains the source and destination IPv4 address information.

Questions:

What is the source IP address?

_____

What is the destination IP address?

_____

f. You can click any line in the middle section to highlight that part of the frame (hex and ASCII) in the **Packet Bytes** pane (bottom section). Click the **Internet Control Message Protocol** line in the middle section and examine what is highlighted in the **Packet Bytes** pane.

Question:

What do the last two highlighted octets spell?

_____

g. Click the next frame in the top section and examine an Echo reply frame. Notice that the source and destination MAC addresses have reversed because this frame was sent from the default gateway router as a reply to the first ping.

Question:

What device and MAC address is displayed as the destination address?

_____

Step 7: Capture packets for a remote host.

a. Click the **Start Capture** icon to start a new Wireshark capture. You will see a pop-up window, asking if you would like to save the previously captured packets to a file before starting a new capture. Click **Continue without Saving**.

b. In a command prompt window, ping **www.cisco.com**.

c. Stop capturing packets.

d. Examine the new data in Wireshark's packet list pane.

Questions:

In the first echo (ping) request frame, what are the source and destination MAC addresses?

Source:

_____

Destination:

_____

What are the source and destination IP addresses contained in the frame's data field?

Source:

_____

Destination:

_____

Compare these addresses to the addresses you received in the previous step. The only address that changed is the destination IP address. Why has the destination IP address changed while the destination MAC address remained the same?

_____

Reflection Question

Wireshark does not display the frame header's preamble field. What does the preamble contain?

_____

Network Layer

This chapter contains no labs or packet tracers.

IPv4 Address Structure

This chapter contains no labs or packet tracers.

Address Resolution

24.1.9 Packet Tracer–Examine the ARP Table

Addressing Table

Device	Interface	MAC Address	Switch Interface
Router0	Gg0/0	0001.6458.2501	G0/1
Router0	S0/0/0	N/A	N/A
Router1	G0/0	00E0.F7B1.8901	G0/1
Router1	S0/0/0	N/A	N/A
10.10.10.2	Wireless	0060.2F84.4AB6	F0/2
10.10.10.3	Wireless	0060.4706.572B	F0/2
172.16.31.2	F0	000C.85CC.1DA7	F0/1
172.16.31.3	F0	0060.7036.2849	F0/2
172.16.31.4	G0	0002.1640.8D75	F0/3

Objectives

- Part 1: Examine an ARP Request
- Part 2: Examine a Switch MAC Address Table
- Part 3: Examine the ARP Process in Remote Communications

Background / Scenario

This activity is optimized for viewing PDUs. The devices are already configured. You will gather PDU information in **Simulation** mode and answer a series of questions about the data you collect.

Instructions

Part 1: Examine an ARP Request

Step 1: Generate ARP requests by pinging 172.16.31.3 from 172.16.31.2.

a. Click **172.16.31.2** and open the **Command Prompt**.

b. Enter the **arp -d** command to clear the ARP table.

c. Enter **Simulation** mode and enter the command **ping 172.16.31.3**. Two PDUs will be generated. The **ping** command cannot complete the ICMP packet without knowing the destination's MAC address. So, the computer sends an ARP broadcast frame to find the MAC address of the destination.

d. Click **Capture/Forward** once. The ARP PDU moves **Switch1** while the ICMP PDU disappears, waiting for the ARP reply. Open the PDU and record the destination MAC address.

Question:

Is this address listed in the table above?

_____

e. Click **Capture/Forward** to move the PDU to the next device.

Question:

How many copies of the PDU did **Switch1** make?

_____

What is the IP address of the device that accepted the PDU?

_____

f. Open the PDU and examine Layer 2.

Question:

What happened to the source and destination MAC addresses?

_____

g. Click **Capture/Forward** until the PDU returns to **172.16.31.2**.

Question:

How many copies of the PDU did the switch make during the ARP reply?

_____

Step 2: Examine the ARP table.

a. Note that the ICMP packet reappears. Open the PDU and examine the MAC addresses.

Question:

Do the MAC addresses of the source and destination align with their IP addresses?

_____

b. Switch back to **Realtime** and the ping completes.

c. Click **172.16.31.2** and enter the **arp –a** command.

Question:

To what IP address does the MAC address entry correspond?

_____

In general, when does an end device issue an ARP request?

_____

Part 2: Examine a Switch MAC Address Table

Step 1: Generate additional traffic to populate the switch MAC address table.

    a. From **172.16.31.2**, enter the ping **172.16.31.4** command.

    b. Click **10.10.10.2** and open the **Command Prompt**.

    c. Enter the **ping 10.10.10.3** command.

    Question:

    How many replies were sent and received?

    _____

Step 2: Examine the MAC address table on the switches.

    a. Click **Switch1** and then the **CLI** tab. Enter the **show mac-address-table** command.

    Question:

    Do the entries correspond to those in the table above?

    _____

    b. Click **Switch0**, followed by the **CLI** tab. Enter the **show mac-address-table** command.

    Questions:

    Do the entries correspond to those in the table above?

    _____

    Why are two MAC addresses associated with one port?

    _____

Part 3: Examine the ARP Process in Remote Communications

Step 1: Generate traffic to produce ARP traffic.

    a. Click **172.16.31.2** and open the **Command Prompt**.

    b. Enter the **ping 10.10.10.1** command.

    c. Type **arp –a**.

    Question:

    What is the IP address of the new ARP table entry?

    _____

    d. Enter **arp -d** to clear the ARP table and switch to **Simulation** mode.

    e. Repeat the ping to **10.10.10.1**.

    Question:

    How many PDUs appear?

    _____

f. Click **Capture/Forward.** Click the PDU that is now at **Switch1.**

Question:

What is the target destination IP destination address of the ARP request?

_____

g. The destination IP address is not **10.10.10.1** router interface's.

Question:

Why?

_____

Step 2: Examine the ARP table on Router1.

a. Switch to **Realtime** mode. Click **Router1** and then the **CLI** tab.

b. Enter **privileged EXEC** mode and then the **show mac-address-table** command.

Question:

How many MAC addresses are in the table? Why?

_____

c. Enter the **show arp** command.

Questions:

Is there an entry for **172.16.31.2**?

_____

What happens to the first ping when the router responds to the ARP request?

_____

24.1.10 Lab–View ARP Traffic in Wireshark

Objectives

Part 1: Capture and Analyze ARP Data in Wireshark

- Start and stop data capture of ping traffic to remote hosts
- Locate the IPv4 and MAC address information in captured PDUs
- Analyze the content of the ARP messages exchanged between devices on the LAN

Part 2: View the ARP Cache Entries on the PC

- Access the Windows Command Prompt
- Use the Windows arp command to view the local ARP table cache on the PC

Background / Scenario

Address Resolution Protocol (ARP) is used by TCP/IP to map a Layer 3 IPv4 address to a Layer 2 MAC address. When an Ethernet frame is transmitted on the network, it must have a destination MAC address. To dynamically discover the MAC address of a known destination, the source device broadcasts an ARP request on the local network. The device that is configured with the destination IPv4 address responds to the request with an ARP reply and the MAC address is recorded in the ARP cache.

Every device on the LAN maintains its own ARP cache. The ARP cache is a small area in RAM that holds the ARP responses. Viewing an ARP cache on a PC displays the IPv4 and the MAC addresses of each device on the LAN with which the PC has exchanged ARP messages.

Wireshark is a software protocol analyzer, or "packet sniffer" application, used for network troubleshooting, analysis, software and protocol development, and education. As data streams travel back and forth over the network, the sniffer "captures" each protocol data unit (PDU) and can decode and analyze its content according to the appropriate protocol specifications.

Wireshark is a useful tool for anyone working with networks and can be used with most labs in the Cisco courses for data analysis and troubleshooting. This lab provides instructions for downloading and installing Wireshark, although it may already be installed. In this lab, you will use Wireshark to capture ARP exchanges on the local network.

Required Resources

- One PC (Choice of operating system with Wireshark installed)
- Additional PC(s) or mobile devices on a local-area network (LAN) can be used to reply to ping requests. If no additional devices are on the LAN, the default gateway address can be used to reply to the ping requests.

Instructions

Part 1: Capture and Analyze Local ARP Data in Wireshark

In this part, you will ping another PC on the LAN and capture ARP requests and replies in Wireshark. You will also look inside the frames captured for specific information. This analysis should help to clarify how packet headers are used to transport data to their destination.

Note: The instructions are written for PCs running Windows OS for your reference.

Step 1: Retrieve your PC's interface addresses.

For this lab, you will need to retrieve your PC's IPv4 address and the MAC address. (The command **ifconfig** for Linux and MAC OS can give you similar results.)

a. Navigate to a Command Prompt window, type **ipconfig /all** at the prompt.

b. Note which network adapter that the PC is using to access the network. Record your PC interface's IPv4 address and MAC address (Physical Address).

```
C:\Users\Student> ipconfig /all

<output omitted>

Wireless LAN adapter Wireless Network Connection:

    Connection-specific DNS Suffix   . :
    Description . . . . . . . . . . . : Intel(R) Centrino(R) Advanced-N
6205
    Physical Address. . . . . . . . . : A4-AE-31-AD-78-4C
    DHCP Enabled. . . . . . . . . . . : Yes
    Autoconfiguration Enabled . . . . : Yes
    Link-local IPv6 Address . . . . . : fe80::f9e7:e41d:a772:f993%11
(Preferred)
    IPv4 Address. . . . . . . . . . . : 192.168.1.8(Preferred)
    Subnet Mask . . . . . . . . . . . : 255.255.255.0
    Lease Obtained. . . . . . . . . . : Thursday, August 04, 2016 05:35:35
PM
    Lease Expires . . . . . . . . . . : Friday, August 05, 2016 05:35:35
PM
    Default Gateway . . . . . . . . . : 192.168.1.1
    DHCP Server . . . . . . . . . . . : 192.168.1.1
    DHCPv6 IAID . . . . . . . . . . . : 245648945
    DHCPv6 Client DUID. . . . . . . . :
00-01-00-01-1B-87-BF-52-A4-4E-31-AD-78-4C
    DNS Servers . . . . . . . . . . . : 192.168.1.1
    NetBIOS over Tcpip. . . . . . . . : Disabled
```

c. At the command prompt of the other PC, enter the command **ipconfig**.

Question:

Record the IPv4 addresses of the default gateway and the other PCs on the LAN.

Note: If you are using a mobile device to ping request reply, search for the directions to find the IP and Wi-Fi MAC addresses for your mobile device.

Note: If you only have one device, the IP address of the other PC can be the default gateway.

Step 2: Start Wireshark and begin capturing data.

a. On your PC, start **Wireshark**.

Note: Alternatively, your installation of Wireshark might also provide a Wireshark Legacy option. This displays Wireshark in the older but widely recognized GUI. The remainder of this lab was completed using the newer GUI.

b. After Wireshark starts, select the network interface you identified with the **ipconfig** command. Enter **arp** in the filter box. This selection configures Wireshark to only display packets that are part of the ARP exchanges between the devices on the local network. Right-click the interface and click **Start capture** to begin the data capture.

Information will start scrolling down the top section in Wireshark. Each line represents a message being sent between a source and destination device on the network.

c. In a **Command Prompt** window, ping the default gateway to test the connectivity to the default gateway address identified in the previous step. (For Linux and MAC OS, use the **ping -c 4 192.168.1.1** command.)

```
C:\Users\Student> ping 192.168.1.1

Pinging 192.168.1.1 with 32 bytes of data:
Reply from 192.168.1.1: bytes=32 time=7ms TTL=64
Reply from 192.168.1.1: bytes=32 time=2ms TTL=64
Reply from 192.168.1.1: bytes=32 time=1ms TTL=64
Reply from 192.168.1.1: bytes=32 time=6ms TTL=64

Ping statistics for 192.168.1.1:
    Packets: Sent = 4, Received = 4, Lost = 0 (0% loss),
Approximate round trip times in milli-seconds:
    Minimum = 1ms, Maximum = 7ms, Average = 4ms
```

d. Ping the IPv4 addresses of other PCs or mobile devices on the LAN that you recorded in the previous step.

Note: If your other device does not reply to your pings, the firewall might be blocking these requests. Search for **unblock firewall** for your operating system on the internet.

e. Stop capturing data by clicking **Stop Capture** (red square icon) on the toolbar.

Step 3: Examine the captured data.

In this step, examine the data generated by the **ping** requests of your team member's PC. Wireshark data is displayed in three sections:

1) The top section displays the list of PDU frames captured with a summary of the IPv4 packet information.

2) The middle section lists PDU information for the frame selected in the top part of the screen and separates a captured PDU frame by its protocol layers.

3) The bottom section displays the raw data of each layer. The raw data is displayed in both hexadecimal and decimal form.

Figure 24-1a   Wireless Network Connection (arp)

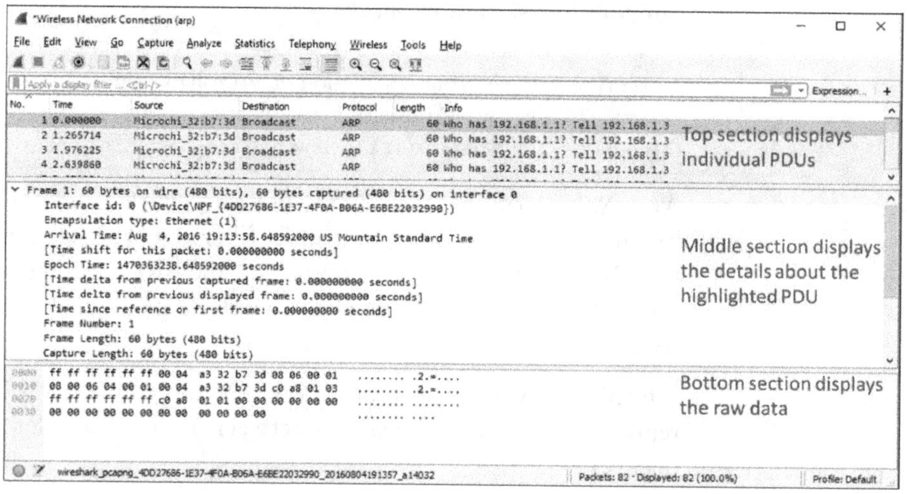

a. Click one of the ARP frames in the top section that has your PC MAC address as the source address in the frame and "broadcast" as the frame's destination.

b. With this PDU frame still selected in the top section, navigate to the middle section. Click the arrow to the left of the Ethernet II row to view the Destination and Source MAC addresses.

Figure 24-1b   Wireless Network Connection (arp)

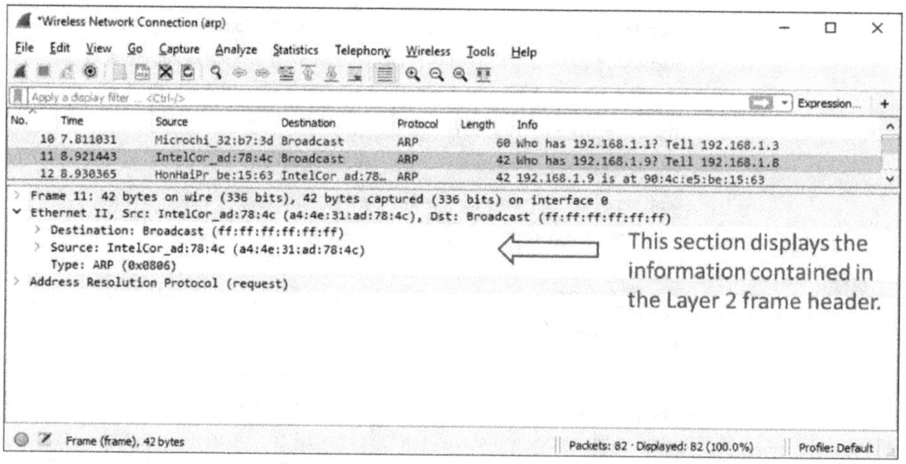

Question:

Does the Source MAC address match your PC's interface?

d. Click the arrow to the left of the **Address Resolution Protocol (request)** row to view the content of the ARP request.

Figure 24-1c   Wireless Network Connection (arp)

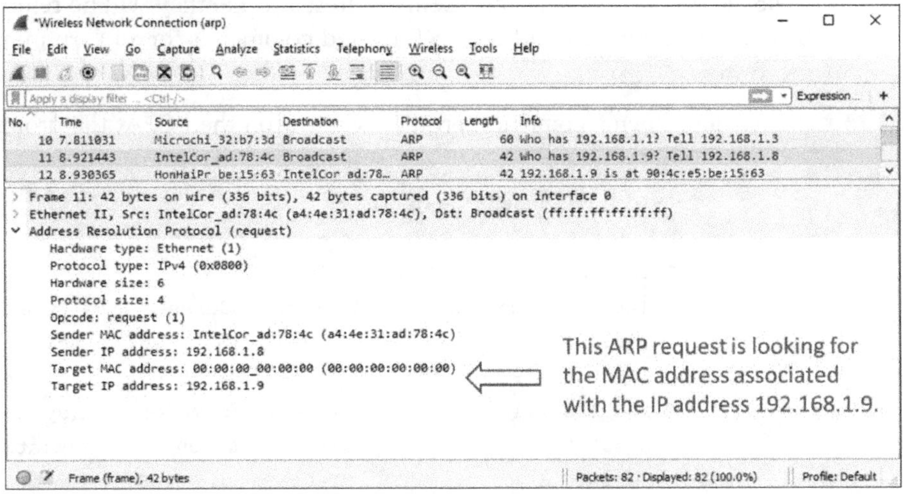

Step 4: Locate the ARP response frame corresponding to the ARP request you highlighted.

a. Using the Target IPv4 address in the ARP request, locate the ARP response frame in the upper section of the Wireshark capture screen.

Question:

What is the IPv4 address of the Target device in your ARP request?

_____

b. Highlight the response frame in the upper section of the Wireshark output. You may have to scroll the window to find the response frame matching the Target IPv4 address identified in the previous step. Expand the **Ethernet II** and **Address Resolution Protocol (response)** rows in the middle section of the screen.

Questions:

Is the ARP response frame a broadcast frame?

_____

What is the frame's destination MAC address of the frame'?

_____

Is this the MAC address of your PC?

_____

What MAC address is the source of the frame?

_____

c. Verify that MAC address matches the MAC address of the device you have selected to reply to ping requests.

Part 2: Examine the ARP Cache Entries on the PC

After the ARP reply is received by the PC, the MAC Address to IPv4 address association is stored in the PC's cache memory. These entries will stay in memory for a short time (from 15 to 45 seconds. If they are not used within that time, they will be removed from cache. (**Note:** Search the internet to find the ARP-related commands for a PC running Linux or MAC operating system.)

a. Open a command prompt window on the PC. At the prompt, enter **arp –a** and press Enter.

```
C:\Users\Student> arp -a

Interface: 192.168.1.8 --- 0xb
  Internet Address         Physical Address        Type
  192.168.1.1              00-37-73-ea-b1-7a        dynamic
  192.168.1.9              90-4c-e5-be-15-63        dynamic
  192.168.1.13             a4-4e-31-ad-78-4c        dynamic
  224.0.0.5                01-00-5e-00-00-05        static
  224.0.0.6                01-00-5e-00-00-06        static
  224.0.0.22               01-00-5e-00-00-16        static
  224.0.0.252              01-00-5e-00-00-fc        static
  224.0.0.253              01-00-5e-00-00-fd        static
  239.255.255.250          01-00-5e-7f-ff-fa        static
  255.255.255.255          ff-ff-ff-ff-ff-ff        static
```

The output of the **arp –a** command displays the entries in the PC's cache. In the example, the PC has entries for the default gateway (192.168.1.1) and two PCs located on the same LAN (192.168.1.9 and 192.168.1.13).

Question:

What is the result of executing the **arp –a** command on your PC?

_____

b. The **arp** command on the Windows PC has another functionality. Enter **arp /?** at the command prompt and press Enter. The **arp** command options enable you to view, add, and remove ARP table entries if necessary.

Question:

Which option deletes an entry from the ARP cache?

_____

c. What would be the result of issuing the **arp –d *** command?

_____

Reflection Questions

1. What is a benefit of keeping ARP cache entries in memory on the source computer?

_____

2. If the destination IPv4 address is not located on the same network as the source host, what MAC address will be used as the destination target MAC address in the frame?

_____

CHAPTER 25

IP Addressing Services

25.1.8 Lab–Observe DNS Resolution

Objectives

- Part 1: Observe the DNS Conversion of a URL to an IP Address
- Part 2: Observe DNS Lookup Using the nslookup Command on a Web Site
- Part 3: Observe DNS Lookup Using the nslookup Command on Mail Servers

Background / Scenario

The Domain Name System (DNS) is invoked when you type a Uniform Resource Locator (URL), such as http://www.cisco.com, into a web browser. The first part of the URL describes which protocol is used. Common protocols are Hypertext Transfer Protocol (HTTP), Hypertext Transfer Protocol over Secure Socket Layer (HTTPS), and File Transfer Protocol (FTP).

DNS uses the second part of the URL, which in this example, is **www.cisco.com**. DNS translates the domain name (**www.cisco.com**) to an IP address to allow the source host to reach the destination server. In this lab, you will observe DNS in action and use the **nslookup** (name server lookup) command to obtain additional DNS information.

Required Resources

One PC (Windows with internet and command prompt access)

Instructions

Part 1: Observe the DNS Conversion of a URL to an IP Address

a. Open a Windows command prompt.

b. At the command prompt, ping the URL for the Internet Corporation for Assigned Names and Numbers (ICANN) at **www.icann.org**. ICANN coordinates the DNS, IP addresses, top-level domain name system management, and root server system management functions. The computer must translate www.icann.org into an IP address to know where to send the Internet Control Message Protocol (ICMP) packets.

The first line of the output displays **www.icann.org** converted to an IP address by DNS. You should be able to see the effect of DNS, even if your institution has a firewall that prevents pinging or if the destination server has prevented you from pinging its web server.

Note: If the domain name is resolved to an IPv6 address, use the **ping -4 www.icann.org** command to translate into an IPv4 address if desired.

```
C:\>  ping www.icann.org


Pinging www.vip.icann.org [2620:0:2d0:200::7] with 32 bytes of data:
Reply from 2620:0:2d0:200::7: time=43ms
Reply from 2620:0:2d0:200::7: time=41ms
Reply from 2620:0:2d0:200::7: time=44ms
Reply from 2620:0:2d0:200::7: time=39ms


Ping statistics for 2620:0:2d0:200::7:
    Packets: Sent = 4, Received = 4, Lost = 0 (0% loss),
Approximate round trip times in milli-seconds:
    Minimum = 39ms, Maximum = 44ms, Average = 41ms


C:\>  ping -4 www.icann.org


Pinging www.vip.icann.org [192.0.32.7] with 32 bytes of data:
Reply from 192.0.32.7: bytes=32 time=41ms TTL=241
Reply from 192.0.32.7: bytes=32 time=42ms TTL=241
Reply from 192.0.32.7: bytes=32 time=42ms TTL=241
Reply from 192.0.32.7: bytes=32 time=43ms TTL=241


Ping statistics for 192.0.32.7:
    Packets: Sent = 4, Received = 4, Lost = 0 (0% loss),
Approximate round trip times in milli-seconds:
    Minimum = 41ms, Maximum = 43ms, Average = 42ms
```

Record the IP addresses for **www.icann.org**.

Close the Windows command prompt

c. Type the IPv4 addresses from step b into a web browser, instead of the URL. Enter **https://192.0.32.7** in the web browser. If your computer has an IPv6 address you can enter the. **https://[2620:0:2d0:200::7]** IPv6 address in to the web browser.

d. Notice that the ICANN home page is displayed without using DNS.

Most people find it easier to remember words, rather than numbers. If you tell someone to go to **www.icann.org**, they can probably remember that. If you told them to go to **192.0.32.7**, they would have a difficult time remembering an IP address. Computers process in numbers. DNS is the process of translating words into numbers. Additionally, there is a second translation that takes place. People think in base-10 numbers. Computers process in base-2 numbers. The base-10 IP address **192.0.32.7** in base-2 numbers is 11000000.00000000.00100000.00000111. What happens if you cut and paste these base-2 numbers into a browser?

---

e. At a command prompt, type **ping www.cisco.com**.

Note: If the domain name is resolved to an IPv6 address, use the **ping -4 www.cisco.com** command to translate into an IPv4 address if desired.

Open a windows command prompt and enter

C:\> **ping www.cisco.com**

```
Pinging origin-www.cisco.com [2600:1408:7:1:9300::90] with 32 bytes of data:
Reply from 2600:1408:7:1:9300::90: time=70ms
Reply from 2600:1408:7:1:9300::90: time=74ms
Reply from 2600:1408:7:1:9300::90: time=72ms
Reply from 2600:1408:7:1:9300::90: time=71ms

Ping statistics for 2600:1408:7:1:9300::90:
    Packets: Sent = 4, Received = 4, Lost = 0 (0% loss),
Approximate round trip times in milli-seconds:
    Minimum = 70ms, Maximum = 74ms, Average = 71ms
```

C:\> **ping -4 www.cisco.com**

```
Pinging e2867.dsca.akamaiedge.net [172.230.155.162] with 32 bytes of data:
Reply from 172.230.155.162: bytes=32 time=7ms TTL=54
Reply from 172.230.155.162: bytes=32 time=6ms TTL=54
Reply from 172.230.155.162: bytes=32 time=7ms TTL=54
Reply from 172.230.155.162: bytes=32 time=6ms TTL=54

Ping statistics for 172.230.155.162:
    Packets: Sent = 4, Received = 4, Lost = 0 (0% loss),
Approximate round trip times in milli-seconds:
    Minimum = 6ms, Maximum = 7ms, Average = 6ms
```

Questions:

When you ping **www.cisco.com**, do you get the same IP address as in the example? Explain.

Type the IP address you obtained when you pinged **www.cisco.com** into a browser. Does the web site display? Explain.

Part 2: Observe DNS Lookup Using the nslookup Command on a Web Site

a. At the command prompt, type the **nslookup** command.

Open a windows command prompt:

C:\> **nslookup**

```
Default Server:  one.one.one.one
```

```
Address:   1.1.1.1


>
```

Question:

What is the default DNS server used?

_____

b. Notice how the command prompt changed to a (**>**) character. This is the **nslookup** prompt. From this prompt, you can enter commands related to DNS.

At the prompt, type **?** to see a list of all the available commands in **nslookup** mode.

c. At the **nslookup** prompt, type **www.cisco.com**.

```
> www.cisco.com
Default Server:   one.one.one.one
Address:   1.1.1.1


Non-authoritative answer:
Name:     e2867.dsca.akamaiedge.net
Addresses:  2600:1404:a:395::b33
            2600:1404:a:38e:::b33
            172.230.155.162
Aliases:  www.cisco.com
          www.cisco.com.akadns.net
          wwwds.cisco.com.edgekey.net
          wwwds.cisco.com.edgekey.net.globalredir.akadns.net
```

Questions:

What is the translated IPv4 address?

_____

Note: The IP address from your location will most likely be different because Cisco uses mirrored servers in various locations around the world.

Is it the same as the IP address shown with the **ping** command?

_____

Under addresses, in addition to the 172.230.155.162 IP address, the following numbers appear: 2600:1404:a:395::b33 and 2600:1404:a:38e:::b33. What are these?

_____

d. At the **nslookup** prompt, type the IP address of the Cisco web server that you just found. You can use **nslookup** to get the domain name of an IP address if you do not know the URL.

```
> 172.230.155.162
Default Server:   one.one.one.one
Address:   1.1.1.1

Name:     a172-230-155-162.deploy.static.akamaitechnologies.com
Address:   172.230.155.162
```

You can use the **nslookup** tool to translate domain names into IP addresses. You can also use it to translate IP addresses into domain names.

Question:

Using the **nslookup** tool, record the IP addresses associated with **www.google.com.**

Part 3: Observe DNS Lookup Using the nslookup Command on Mail Servers

a. At the nslookup prompt, type **set type=mx** to use **nslookup** to identify mail servers.

> **set type=mx**

b. At the nslookup prompt, type **cisco.com.**

```
> cisco.com

Server:   one.one.one.one

Address:  1.1.1.1

Non-authoritative answer:

cisco.com        MX preference = 20, mail exchanger = rcdn-mx-01.cisco.com

cisco.com        MX preference = 30, mail exchanger = aer-mx-01.cisco.com

cisco.com        MX preference = 10, mail exchanger = alln-mx-01.cisco.com
```

A fundamental principle of network design is redundancy (more than one mail server is configured). If one of the mail servers is unreachable, the computer making the query tries the second mail server. Email administrators determine which mail server is contacted first by using **MX preference**. The mail server with the lowest **MX preference** is contacted first.

Question:

Based upon the output above, which mail server will be contacted first when the email is sent to **cisco.com?**

c. At the **nslookup** prompt, type **exit** to return to the regular PC command prompt.

d. At the PC command prompt, type **ipconfig /all.**

Question:

Write the IP addresses of all the DNS servers your school uses.

Reflection Question

What is the fundamental purpose of DNS?

CHAPTER 26

Transport Layer

26.8.1 Packet Tracer–TCP and UDP Communications

Objectives

- Part 1: Generate Network Traffic in Simulation Mode
- Part 2: Examine the Functionality of the TCP and UDP Protocols

Background

This simulation activity is intended to provide a foundation for understanding TCP and UDP in detail. Packet Tracer Simulation mode provides you with the ability to view the state of different PDUs as they travel through the network.

Packet Tracer Simulation mode enables you to view each of the protocols and the associated PDUs. The steps outlined below lead you through the process of requesting network services using various applications available on a client PC. You will explore the functionality of the TCP and UDP protocols, multiplexing, and the function of port numbers in determining which local application requested or sent the data. Packet Tracer will not score this activity.

Instructions

Part 1: Generate Network Traffic in Simulation Mode and View Multiplexing

Step 1: Generate traffic to populate Address Resolution Protocol (ARP) tables.

Perform the following task to reduce the amount of network traffic viewed in the simulation.

a. Click **MultiServer**, click the **Desktop** tab, and select **Command Prompt**.

b. Enter the **ping -n 1 192.168.1.255** command. You are pinging the broadcast address for the client LAN. The command option will send only one ping request, rather than the usual four. This will take a few seconds as every device on the network responds to the ping request from MultiServer.

c. Close the **MultiServer** window.

Step 2: Generate web (HTTP) traffic.

a. Switch to **Simulation** mode.

b. Click **HTTP Client** and open a web browser from the desktop.

c. In the URL field, enter **192.168.1.254** and click **Go**. Envelopes (PDUs) will appear in the topology window.

d. Minimize, but do not close, the **HTTP Client** configuration window.

Step 3: Generate FTP traffic.

    a. Click **FTP Client** and open the **Command Prompt** from the desktop.

    b. Enter the ftp **192.168.1.254** command. PDUs will appear in the simulation window.

    c. Minimize, but do not close, the **FTP Client** configuration window.

Step 4: Generate DNS traffic.

    a. Click **DNS Client** and open the **Command Prompt**.

    b. Enter the **nslookup multiserver.pt.ptu** command. A PDU will appear in the simulation window.

    c. Minimize, but do not close, the **DNS Client** configuration window.

Step 5: Generate Email traffic.

    a. Click **E-Mail Client** and open the **E Mail** tool from the desktop.

    b. Click **Compose** and enter the following information:

        1) **To:** user@multiserver.pt.ptu

        2) **Subject:** personalize the subject line

        3) **E-Mail Body:** personalize the email

    c. Click **Send.**

    d. Minimize, but do not close, the **E-Mail Client** configuration window.

Step 6: Verify that the traffic is generated and ready for simulation.

There should now be PDU entries in the simulation panel for each of the client computers.

Step 7: Examine multiplexing as the traffic crosses the network.

You will now use the **Capture/Forward** button in the simulation panel to observe the different protocols traveling on the network.

Note: The **Capture/Forward** button appears as a small arrow pointing to the right with a vertical bar next to it: >|.

---

    a. Click **Capture/Forward** once. All of the PDUs travel to the switch.

    b. Click **Capture/Forward** six times and watch the PDUs from the different hosts as they travel on the network. Note that only one PDU can cross a wire in each direction at any given time.

Questions:

What is this called?

A variety of PDUs appears in the event list in the simulation panel. What is the meaning of the different colors?

Part 2: Examine the Functionality of the TCP and UDP Protocols

Step 1: Examine HTTP traffic as the clients communicate with the server.

    a. Click **Reset Simulation**.

    b. Filter the traffic currently displayed to only **HTTP** and **TCP PDUs**. To filter the traffic currently displayed:

       1) Click **Edit Filters** and toggle the **Show All/None** button.

       2) Select **HTTP** and **TCP**. Click the red X in the upper right-hand corner of the **Edit Filters** box to close it. **Visible Events** should now display only **HTTP** and **TCP PDUs**.

    c. Open the browser on HTTP Client and enter **192.168.1.254** in the **URL** field. Click **Go** to connect to the server over HTTP. Minimize the HTTP client window.

    d. Click **Capture/Forward** until you see a PDU appear for HTTP. Note that the color of the envelope in the topology window matches the color code of the HTTP PDU in the simulation panel.

    Question:

    Why did it take so long for the HTTP PDU to appear?

    e. Click the PDU envelope to show the PDU details. Click the **Outbound PDU Details** tab and scroll down to the second to the last section.

    Questions:

    What is the section labeled?

    Are these communications considered reliable?

    What are the **SRC PORT, DEST PORT, SEQUENCE NUM,** and **ACK NUM** values?

    f. Look at the value in the **Flags** field, which is located next to the **Window** field. The values to the right of the "b" represent the TCP flags set for this stage of the data conversation. Each of the six places corresponds to a flag. The presence of a "1" in any place indicates that the flag is set. More than one flag can be set at a time. The values for the flags are shown below.

Flag Place	6	5	4	3	2	1
Value	URG	ACK	PSH	RST	SYN	FIN

    Question:

    Which TCP flags are set in this PDU?

g. Close the PDU and click **Capture/Forward** until a PDU with a checkmark returns to the **HTTP Client**.

h. Click the PDU envelope and select **Inbound PDU Details**.

Question:

How are the port and sequence numbers different than before?

_____

i. Click the HTTP PDU, which the **HTTP Client** has prepared to send to the **MultiServer**. This is the beginning of the HTTP communication. Click this second PDU envelope and select **Outbound PDU Details**.

Question:

What information is now listed in the TCP section? How are the port and sequence numbers different from the previous two PDUs?

_____

j. Reset the simulation.

Step 2: Examine FTP traffic as the clients communicate with the server.

a. Open the command prompt on the FTP Client desktop. Initiate an FTP connection by entering **ftp 192.168.1.254**.

b. In the simulation panel, change **Edit Filters** to display only **FTP** and **TCP**.

c. Click **Capture/Forward**. Click the second PDU envelope to open it.

d. Click the **Outbound PDU Details** tab and scroll down to the TCP section.

Question:

Are these communications considered reliable?

_____

d. Record the **SRC PORT**, **DEST PORT**, **SEQUENCE NUM**, and **ACK NUM** values.

Question:

What is the value in the flag field?

_____

e. Close the PDU and click **Capture/Forward** until a PDU returns to the **FTP Client** with a checkmark.

f. Click the PDU envelope and select **Inbound PDU Details**.

Question:

How are the port and sequence numbers different than before?

_____

Click the **Outbound PDU Details** tab.

Question:

How are the port and sequence numbers different from the previous results?

_____

h. Close the PDU and click **Capture/Forward** until a second PDU returns to the **FTP Client.** The PDU is a different color.

i. Open the PDU and select **Inbound PDU Details.** Scroll down past the TCP section.

Question:

What is the message from the server?

_____

j. Click **Reset Simulation.**

Step 3: Examine DNS traffic as the clients communicate with the server.

a. Repeat the steps in Part 1 to create DNS traffic.

b. In the simulation panel, change **Edit Filters** to display only **DNS** and **UDP.**

c. Click the PDU envelope to open it.

d. Look at the OSI Model details for the outbound PDU.

Question:

What is the Layer 4 protocol?

_____

Are these communications considered reliable?

_____

e. Open the **Outbound PDU Details** tab and find the UDP section of the PDU formats. Record the **SRC PORT** and **DEST PORT** values.

Question:

Why are there no sequence and acknowledgment numbers?

_____

f. Close the **PDU** and click **Capture/Forward** until a PDU with a checkmark returns to the **DNS Client.**

g. Click the PDU envelope and select **Inbound PDU Details.**

Question:

How are the port and sequence numbers different than before?

_____

What is the last section of the **PDU** called? What is the IP address for the name **multiserver.pt.ptu?**

_____

h. Click **Reset Simulation.**

Step 4: Examine email traffic as the clients communicate with the server.

a. Repeat the steps in Part 1 to send an email to user@multiserver.pt.ptu.

b. In the simulation panel, change **Edit Filters** to display only **POP3, SMTP,** and **TCP.**

c. Click the first PDU envelope to open it.

d. Click the **Outbound PDU Details** tab and scroll down to the last section.

Questions:

What transport layer protocol does email traffic use?

_____

Are these communications considered reliable?

_____

e. Record the **SRC PORT, DEST PORT, SEQUENCE NUM,** and **ACK NUM** values. What is the flag field value?

_____

f. Close the **PDU** and click **Capture/Forward** until a PDU returns to the **E-Mail Client** with a checkmark.

g. Click the TCP PDU envelope and select **Inbound PDU Details.**

Question:

How are the port and sequence numbers different than before?

_____

h. Click the **Outbound PDU Details** tab.

Question:

How are the port and sequence numbers different from the previous two results?

_____

i. There is a second **PDU** in a different color that **E-Mail Client** has prepared to send to **MultiServer.** This is the beginning of the email communication. Click this second PDU envelope and select **Outbound PDU Details.**

Questions:

How are the port and sequence numbers different from the previous two **PDUs?**

_____

What email protocol is associated with TCP port 25? What protocol is associated with TCP port 110?

_____

CHAPTER 27

The Cisco IOS Command Line

Packet Tracer
☐ Activity

27.2.6 Packet Tracer–Navigate the IOS

Objectives

- Part 1: Establish Basic Connections, Access the CLI, and Explore Help
- Part 2: Explore EXEC Modes
- Part 3: Set the Clock

Background / Scenario

In this activity, you will practice the skills necessary for navigating the Cisco IOS, such as different user access modes, various configuration modes, and common commands used on a regular basis. You will also practice accessing the context-sensitive **Help** by configuring the **clock** command.

Instructions

Part 1: Establish Basic Connections, Access the CLI, and Explore Help

Step 1: Connect PC1 to S1 using a console cable.

    a. Click the **Connections** icon (the one that looks like a lightning bolt) in the lower-left corner of the **Packet Tracer** window.

    b. Select the light-blue **Console** cable by clicking it. The mouse pointer will change to what appears to be a connector with a cable dangling from it.

    c. Click **PC1**. A window displays an option for an **RS-232** connection. Connect the cable to the RS-232 port.

    d. Drag the other end of the console connection to the S1 switch and click the switch to access the connection list.

    e. Select the **Console** port to complete the connection.

Step 2: Establish a terminal session with S1.

    a. Click **PC1** and then select the **Desktop** tab.

    b. Click the **Terminal** application icon. Verify that the **Port Configuration** default settings are correct.

    Question:

    What is the setting for bits per second?

    _____

    c. Click **OK**.

d. The screen that appears may have several messages displayed. Somewhere on the screen, there should be a **Press RETURN to get started!** message. Press **ENTER.**

Question:

What is the prompt displayed on the screen?

_____

Step 3: Explore the IOS Help.

a. The IOS can provide **Help** for commands depending on the level accessed. The prompt currently displayed is called **User EXEC**, and the device is waiting for a command. The most basic form of **Help** is to type a question mark (**?**) at the prompt to display a list of commands.

```
S1> ?
```
Question:

Which command begins with the letter "C"?

_____

b. At the prompt, type **t** and then a question mark (**?**).

```
S1> t?
```
Question:

Which commands are displayed?

_____

At the prompt, type **te** and then a question mark (**?**).

```
S1> te?
```
Question:

Which commands are displayed?

_____

This type of **Help** is known as context-sensitive **Help**. It provides more information as the commands are expanded.

Part 2: Explore EXEC Modes

In this part of the activity, you will switch to privileged EXEC mode and issue additional commands.

Step 1: Enter privileged EXEC mode.

a. At the prompt, type a question mark (**?**).

```
S1> ?
```
Question:

What information is displayed for the **enable** command?

_____

b. Type **en** and press the **Tab** key.

```
S1> en<Tab>
```

Question:

What displays after pressing the **Tab** key?

This is called command completion (or tab completion). When part of a command is typed, the **Tab** key can be used to complete the partial command. If the characters typed are enough to make the command unique, as in the case of the **enable** command, the remaining portion of the command is displayed.

Question:

What would happen if you typed **te<Tab>** at the prompt?

---

c. Enter the **enable** command and press **ENTER**.

Question:

How does the prompt change?

---

d. When prompted, type the question mark (**?**).

```
S1# ?
```

One command starts with the letter "C" in user EXEC mode.

Question:

How many commands are displayed now that privileged EXEC mode is active? (**Hint:** you could type c? to list just the commands beginning with "C".)

Step 2: Enter Global Configuration mode

a. When in privileged EXEC mode, one of the commands starting with the letter "C" is **configure**. Type either the full command or enough of the command to make it unique. Press the <**Tab**> key to issue the command and press **Enter**.

```
S1# configure
```

Question:

What is the message that is displayed?

---

b. Press **Enter** to accept the default parameter enclosed in brackets: [**terminal**].

Question:

How does the prompt change?

---

c. This is called global configuration mode. This mode will be explored further in upcoming activities and labs. For now, return to privileged EXEC mode by typing **end, exit,** or **Ctrl-Z.**

```
S1(config)# exit
S1#
```

Part 3: Set the Clock

Step 1: Use the clock command.

a. Use the **clock** command to further explore **Help** and command syntax. Type **show clock** at the privileged EXEC prompt.

```
S1# show clock
```

Question:

What information is displayed? What is the year that is displayed?

_____

b. Use the context-sensitive **Help** and the **clock** command to set the time on the switch to the current time. Enter the command **clock** and press **Enter.**

```
S1# clock<ENTER>
```

Question

What information is displayed?

_____

c. The **% Incomplete command** message is returned by the IOS. This indicates that the **clock** command needs more parameters. When more information is needed, **Help** can be provided by typing a space after the command and the question mark (**?**).

```
S1# clock ?
```

Question:

What information is displayed?

_____

d. Set the clock using the **clock set** command. Proceed through the command one step at a time.

```
S1# clock set ?
```

Questions:

What information is being requested?

_____

What would have been displayed if only the **clock set** command had been entered, and no request for **Help** was made by using the question mark (**?**)

_____

e. Based on the information requested by issuing the **clock set ?** command, enter a time of 3:00 p.m. by using the 24-hour format of 15:00:00. Check to see if more parameters are needed.

```
S1# clock set 15:00:00 ?
```

The output returns a request for more information:

```
<1-31>  Day of the month
MONTH   Month of the year
```

f. Attempt to set the date to 01/31/2035 using the format requested. It may be necessary to request additional **Help** using context-sensitive **Help** to complete the process. When finished, issue the **show clock** command to display the clock setting. The resulting command output should display as:

```
S1# show clock
*15:0:4.869 UTC Wed Jan 31 2035
```

g. If you were not successful, try the following command to obtain the output above:

```
S1# clock set 15:00:00 31 Jan 2035
```

Step 2: Explore additional command messages.

a. The IOS provides various outputs for incorrect or incomplete commands. Continue to use the **clock** command to explore additional messages that may be encountered as you learn to use the IOS.

b. Issue the following commands and record the messages:

```
S1# cl<enter>
```

Questions:

What information was returned?

_____

```
S1# clock
```

What information was returned?

_____

```
S1# clock set 25:00:00
```

What information was returned?

_____

```
S1# clock set 15:00:00 32
```

What information was returned?

_____

Close the configuration window.

27.3.3 Packet Tracer–Use Cisco IOS Show Commands

Objectives

- Use Cisco IOS **show** commands

Background / Scenario

The Cisco IOS **show** commands are used extensively when working with Cisco equipment. In this activity, you will use the **show** commands on a router located at an ISP.

Instructions

Part 1: Connect to the ISP Cisco 4321 Router

In this part, you will use the terminal emulation software on ISP PC to connect to the Cisco 4321 router.

   a. Click **ISP PC**.

   b. Click the **Desktop** tab. Select **Terminal**. Review the terminal configuration and click **OK** to continue.

   c. The **ISPRouter >** prompt indicates are in user EXEC mode. Press **Enter** if the prompt did not display.

Part 2: Explore the show Commands

Use the information displayed by these **show** commands to answer the following questions.

Step 1: Explore show commands in User EXEC mode.

   Open configuration window.

   a. Type **show ?** at the prompt.

   Question:

   List a few more **show** commands available in the user EXEC mode.

_____

   b. Enter **show arp** at the prompt.

   Question:

   What MAC address and the IP address are listed?

_____

   c. Enter **show flash** at the prompt.

   Question:

   What IOS image is listed?

_____

d. Enter **show ip route** at the prompt.

Question:

How many routes are listed in the table?

_____

e. Enter **show interfaces** at the prompt.

Question:

Which interfaces are running?

Interface	Status	Protocol
GigabitEthernet 0/0/0	Up	
GigabitEthernet 0/0/1		Down
Serial0/1/0	Down	
Serial0/1/1		

f. Enter **show ip interface** at the prompt.

Question:

According to the **show ip interface** output, which interface is connected?

_____

g. Enter **show version** at the prompt.

Question:

What technology package is enabled currently on the router?

_____

h. Enter **show protocols** at the prompt.

Question:

Which protocols are enabled currently on the router?

_____

i. Enter **show running-config** at the prompt.

Question:

What is the output?

_____

Step 2: Explore the show commands in privileged EXEC mode.

a. Enter **enable** at the prompt to enter the privileged EXEC mode.

Question:

What are some additional **show** commands in this mode?

_____

b.   Enter **show running-config** at the prompt.

Question:

What is the output?

_____

Close the configuration window.

CHAPTER 28

Build a Small Cisco Network

28.1.4 Packet Tracer–Implement Basic Connectivity

Addressing Table

Device	Interface	IP Address	Subnet Mask
S1	VLAN 1	192.168.1.253	255.255.255.0
S2	VLAN 1	192.168.1.254	255.255.255.0
PC1	NIC	192.168.1.1	255.255.255.0
PC2	NIC	192.168.1.2	255.255.255.0

Objectives

- Part 1: Perform a Basic Configuration on S1 and S2
- Part 2: Configure the PCs
- Part 3: Configure the Switch Management Interface

Background / Scenario

In this activity, you will first perform basic switch configurations. Then, you will implement basic connectivity by configuring IP addressing on the switches and PCs. When the IP addressing configuration is complete, you will use various **show** commands to verify configurations and use the **ping** command to verify basic connectivity between devices.

Instructions

Part 1: Perform SVI Configuration on S1 and S2

Step 1: Configure S1 with a hostname.

    a. Click **S1**, and then click the **CLI** tab.

    b. Enter the privileged EXEC mode. Then enter the global configuration mode.

```
Switch> enable
Switch# configure terminal
Enter configuration commands, one per line.  End with CNTL/Z.
```

    c. Configure the hostname as **S1**.

```
Switch(config)# hostname S1
S1(config)#
```

Step 2: Configure S1 with an IP address.

Switches can be used without any configurations. Switches forward information from one port to another based on Media Access Control (MAC) addresses.

    Question:

    Why does a switch need an IP address?

a. In the global configuration mode, enter the following commands to configure S1 with an IP address in VLAN 1.

```
S1(config)# interface vlan 1
S1(config-if)# ip address 192.168.1.253 255.255.255.0
S1(config-if)# no shutdown
%LINEPROTO-5-UPDOWN: Line protocol on Interface Vlan1, changed state to up
```

Question:

What does the **no shutdown** command do?

_____

b. Exit the configuration mode and save the configuration.

```
S1(config-if)# end
S1#
S1# copy running-config startup-config
Destination filename [startup-config]?
Building configuration...
[OK]
```

c. Verify the IP address configuration on S1.

```
S1# show ip interface brief
<output omitted>
  Vlan1                    192.168.1.253    YES manual up                    up
```

Step 3: Configure S2 with a hostname and IP address.

In this step, you will configure **S2** with a hostname and IP address.

a. Click **S2**. On the **CLI** tab, enter the global configuration mode.

b. Configure the **S2** switch with a hostname using the information according to the Addressing Table at the beginning of the chapter.

c. Using the information in the Addressing Table, repeat the same process to configure the switch **S2** switch with an IP address.

d. Exit the configuration mode. Verify the IP address configuration on S2.

```
S2# show ip interface brief
<output omitted>
  Vlan1                    192.168.1.254    YES manual up                    up
```

e. Save the configuration file to NVRAM. Enter the **copy running-config startup-config** command to save the configuration.

Part 2: Configure the PCs

In this part, you will configure **PC1** and **PC2** with IP addresses and verify network connectivity.

Step 1: Configure both PCs with IP addresses.

a. Click **PC1**, and then click the **Desktop** tab.

b. Click **IP Configuration**. In the Addressing Table at the beginning of this chapter, you can see that the IP address for PC1 is supposed to be **192.168.1.1** and the subnet mask should be **255.255.255.0**. Enter this information for **PC1** in the **IP Configuration** window.

c. Repeat the previous steps for **PC2**. Use the IP address listed in the Address Table for **PC2**.

Step 2: Test connectivity from the PCs.

a. Click **PC1**. Close the **IP Configuration** window if it is still open. On the **Desktop** tab, click **Command Prompt**.

b. Enter the **ping** command and the IP address for **S1**.

```
Packet Tracer PC Command Line 1.0
PC> ping 192.168.1.253
```

Question:

Were you successful? Explain.

---

f. From **PC1**, ping **S2** and **PC2**.

g. Repeat the pings to **S1**, **S2**, and **PC1** from **PC2**.

All pings should be successful. If your first ping result is 80 percent, retry; it should now be 100 percent. You will learn why a ping may fail the first time later in your studies. If you cannot ping any of the devices, check your configuration for errors.

Step 3: Verify network connectivity from the switches.

Network connectivity can be verified using the **ping** command. It is very important that connectivity exists throughout the network.

a. From **S1**, ping the other devices in the network. The ping to **PC1** is displayed below as an example.

```
S1> ping 192.168.1.1
Type escape sequence to abort.
Sending 5, 100-byte ICMP Echos to 192.168.1.1, timeout is 2 seconds:
!!!!!
Success rate is 100 percent (5/5), round-trip min/avg/max = 0/0/1 ms
```

b. From **S2**, ping the other devices in the network.

All pings should be successful. If your first ping result is 80 percent, retry; it should now be 100 percent. You will learn why a ping may fail the first time later in your studies. If you cannot ping any of the devices, check your configuration for errors.

28.2.4 Packet Tracer–Configure Initial Router Settings

Objectives

- Part 1: Verify the Default Router Configuration
- Part 2: Configure and Verify the Initial Router Configuration
- Part 3: Save the Running Configuration File

Background / Scenario

In this activity, you will perform basic router configuration tasks. You will secure access to the CLI and console port using encrypted and plain-text passwords. You will also configure messages for users who are logging into the router. These banners warn unauthorized users that access is prohibited. Finally, you will verify and save your running configuration.

Instructions

Part 1: Verify the Default Router Configuration

Step 1: Establish a console connection to R1.

a. Choose a **Console** cable from the available connections.

b. Click **PCA** and select **RS 232**.

c. Click **R1** and select **Console**.

d. Click **PCA**, and from the **Desktop** tab, select **Terminal**.

e. Click **OK** and press **Enter**. You can now configure **R1**.

Step 2: Enter privileged mode and examine the current configuration.

You can access all the router commands from privileged EXEC mode. However, because many of the privileged commands configure operating parameters, privileged access should be password-protected to prevent unauthorized use.

a. Enter privileged EXEC mode by entering the **enable** command.

```
Router> enable
Router#
```

Notice that the prompt changed in the configuration to reflect privileged EXEC mode.

b. Enter the **show running-config** command.

```
Router# show running-config
```

Questions:

What is the router's hostname?

_____

How many Fast Ethernet interfaces does the router have?

_____

How many Gigabit Ethernet interfaces does the router have?

How many serial interfaces does the router have?

What is the range of values shown for the vty lines?

c. Display the current contents of NVRAM.

```
Router# show startup-config
startup-config is not present
```

Question:

Why does the router respond with the **startup-config is not present** message?

Part 2: Configure and Verify the Initial Router Configuration

To configure parameters on a router, you may be required to move between various configuration modes. Notice how the prompt changes as you navigate through the IOS configuration modes.

Step 1: Configure the initial settings on R1.

Note: If you have difficulty remembering the commands, refer to the content for this topic.

a. Configure **R1** as the hostname.

b. Configure the **Message of the day** text: **Unauthorized access is strictly prohibited.**

c. Encrypt all plain text passwords.

Use the following passwords:

1) Privileged EXEC, encrypted: itsasecret

2) Console: letmein

Step 2: Verify the initial settings on R1.

a. Verify the initial settings by viewing the configuration for **R1**.

Question:

What command do you use?

b. Exit the current console session until you see the following message:

```
R1 con0 is now available
Press RETURN to get started.
```

c. Press **ENTER**; you should see the following message:

```
Unauthorized access is strictly prohibited.
User Access Verification
Password:
```

Questions:

Why should every router have a message-of-the-day (MOTD) banner?

_____

If you are not prompted for a password before reaching the user EXEC prompt, what console line command did you forget to configure?

_____

d. Enter the passwords necessary to return to privileged EXEC mode.

Questions:

If you configure any more passwords on the router, are they displayed in the configuration file as plain text or in encrypted form? Explain.

_____

Part 3: Save the Running Configuration File

Step 1: Save the configuration file to NVRAM.

a. You have configured the initial settings for **R1**. Now back up the running configuration file to NVRAM to ensure that the changes made are not lost if the system is rebooted or loses power.

Questions:

What command did you enter to save the configuration to NVRAM?

_____

What is the shortest, unambiguous version of this command?

_____

Which command displays the contents of the NVRAM?

_____

b. Verify that all the parameters configured are recorded. If not, analyze the output and determine which commands were not executed or entered incorrectly. You can also click **Check Results** in the instruction window.

Step 2: Optional: Save the startup configuration file to flash.

Although you will be learning more about managing the flash storage in a router in later chapters, you may be interested to know that, as an added backup procedure, you can save your startup configuration file to flash. By default, the router still loads the startup configuration from NVRAM, but if NVRAM becomes corrupt, you can restore the startup configuration by copying it over from flash.

Complete the following steps to save the startup configuration to flash.

a. Examine the contents of flash using the **show flash** command:

```
R1# show flash
```

Questions:

How many files are currently stored in flash?

_____

Which of these files would you guess is the IOS image?

_____

Why do you think this file is the IOS image?

_____

b. Save the startup configuration file to flash using the following commands:

```
R1# copy startup-config flash
Destination filename [startup-config]
```

The router prompts you to store the file in flash using the name in brackets. If the answer is yes, then press **Enter**; if not, type an appropriate name and press **Enter**.

c. Use the **show flash** command to verify the startup configuration file is now stored in flash.

28.3.6 Packet Tracer–Configure SSH

Addressing Table

Device	Interface	IP Address	Subnet Mask
S1	VLAN 1	10.10.10.2	255.255.255.0
PC1	NIC	10.10.10.10	255.255.255.0

Objectives

- Part 1: Secure Passwords
- Part 2: Encrypt Communications
- Part 3: Verify SSH Implementation

Background / Scenario

SSH should replace Telnet for management connections. Telnet uses insecure plain text communications. SSH provides security for remote connections by providing strong encryption of all transmitted data between devices. In this activity, you will secure a remote switch with password encryption and SSH.

Instructions

Part 1: Secure Passwords

a. Using the command prompt on **PC1**, Telnet to **S1**. The user EXEC and privileged EXEC password is **cisco**.

```
PC> telnet 10.10.10.2
Trying 10.10.10.2 ...Open


User Access Verification

Password:
S1> en
Password:
S1#
```

b. Save the current configuration so any mistakes you might make can be reversed by toggling the power for **S1**.

```
S1# copy running-config startup-config
Destination filename [startup-config]?
Building configuration...
[OK]
```

c. Show the current configuration and note that the passwords are in plain text.

d. In the global configuration mode, enter the command that encrypts plain text passwords:

```
S1(config)# service password-encryption
```

e. Verify that the passwords are encrypted.

Part 2: Encrypt Communications

Step 1: Set the IP domain name and generate secure keys.

It is generally not safe to use Telnet because data is transferred in plain text. Therefore, use SSH whenever it is available.

a. Configure the domain name to be netacad.pka.

```
S1(config)# ip domain-name netacad.pka
```

b. Secure keys are needed to encrypt the data. Generate the RSA keys using a 1024-key length.

```
S1(config)# crypto key generate rsa
The name for the keys will be: S1.netacad.pka
Choose the size of the key modulus in the range of 360 to 2048 for your
    General Purpose Keys. Choosing a key modulus greater than 512 may take
    a few minutes.

How many bits in the modulus [512]: 1024
% Generating 1024 bit RSA keys, keys will be non-exportable...[OK]
```

Step 2: Create an SSH user and reconfigure the VTY lines for SSH-only access.

a. Create an **administrator** user with **cisco** as the secret password.

```
S1(config)# username administrator secret cisco
```

b. Configure the VTY lines to check the local username database for login credentials and to only allow SSH for remote access. Remove the existing vty line password.

```
S1(config)# line vty 0 15
S1(config-line)# login local
S1(config-line)# transport input ssh
S1(config-line)# no password cisco
```

Part 3: Verify SSH Implementation

a. Exit the Telnet session and attempt to log back in using Telnet. The attempt should fail.

b. Attempt to log in using SSH. Type **ssh** and press **Enter** without any parameters to reveal the command usage instructions. Hint: The -l option is the letter "L", not the number 1.

c. Upon successful log in, enter privileged EXEC mode and save the configuration. If you were unable to successfully access **S1**, toggle the power and begin again at Part 1.

Packet Tracer
☐ Activity

28.4.5 Packet Tracer–Troubleshoot Default Gateway Issues

Addressing Table

Device	Interface	IP Address	Subnet Mask	Default Gateway
R1	G0/0	192.168.10.1	255.255.255.0	N/A
	G0/1	192.168.11.1	255.255.255.0	N/A
S1	VLAN 1	192.168.10.2	255.255.255.0	
S2	VLAN 1	192.168.11.2	255.255.255.0	
PC1	NIC	192.168.10.10	255.255.255.0	
PC2	NIC	192.168.10.11	255.255.255.0	
PC3	NIC	192.168.11.10	255.255.255.0	
PC4	NIC	192.168.11.11	255.255.255.0	

Objectives

- Part 1: Verify Network Documentation and Isolate Problems
- Part 2: Implement, Verify, and Document Solutions

Background / Scenario

For a device to communicate across multiple networks, it must be configured with an IP address, subnet mask, and a default gateway. The default gateway is used when the host wants to send a packet to a device on another network. The default gateway address is generally the address of the router interface, which is attached to the local network that the host is connected to. In this activity, you will finish documenting the network. You will then verify the network documentation by testing end-to-end connectivity and troubleshooting issues. The troubleshooting method you will use consists of the following steps:

a. Verify the network documentation and use tests to isolate problems.

b. Determine an appropriate solution for a given problem.

c. Implement the solution.

d. Test to verify the problem is resolved.

e. Document the solution.

Throughout your CCNA studies, you will encounter different descriptions of the troubleshooting method, as well as different ways to test and document issues and solutions. This is intentional. There is no set standard or template for troubleshooting. Each organization develops unique processes and documentation standards (even if that process is "we don't have one"). However, all effective troubleshooting methodologies generally include the steps above.

Note: If you are proficient with default gateway configurations, this activity might seem more involved than it should be. You can, most likely, quickly discover and solve all the connectivity issues faster than following these procedures. However, as you proceed in your studies, the networks and problems you encounter will become increasingly more complex. In such situations, the only effective way to isolate and solve issues is to use a methodical approach such as the one used in this activity.

Instructions

Part 1: Verify Network Documentation and Isolate Problems

In Part 1 of this activity, complete the documentation and perform connectivity tests to discover issues. In addition, you will determine an appropriate solution for implementation in Part 2.

Step 1: Verify the network documentation and isolate any problems.

a. Before you can effectively test a network, you must have complete documentation. Notice in the Addressing Table that some information is missing. Complete the Addressing Table by filling in the missing default gateway information for the switches and PCs.

b. Test connectivity to devices on the same network. By isolating and correcting any local access issues, you can better test remote connectivity with the confidence that local connectivity is operational.

A verification plan can be as simple as a list of connectivity tests. Use the following tests to verify local connectivity and isolate any access issues. The first issue is already documented, but you must implement and verify the solution during Part 2.

Testing and Verification Documentation

Test	Successful?	Issues	Solution	Verified
PC1 to PC2	No	IP address on PC1	Change PC1 IP address	
PC1 to S1				
PC1 to R1				

Note: The Testing and Verification Documentation table is an example; you must create your own document. You can use paper and pencil to draw a table, or you can use a text editor or spreadsheet. Consult your instructor if you need further guidance.

c. Test connectivity to remote devices (such as from PC1 to PC4) and document any problems. This is frequently referred to as *end-to-end connectivity*. This means that all devices in a network have the full connectivity allowed by the network policy.

Note: Remote connectivity testing may not be possible yet because you must first resolve local connectivity issues. After you have solved those issues, return to this step and test connectivity between networks.

Step 2: Determine an appropriate solution for the problem.

    a. Using your knowledge of how networks operate and your device configuration skills, search for the cause of the problem. For example, **S1** is not the cause of the connectivity issue between **PC1** and **PC2**. The link lights are green, and no configuration on **S1** would cause traffic to not pass between PC1 and PC2. So the problem must be with **PC1**, **PC2**, or both.

    b. Verify the device addressing to ensure it matches the network documentation. For example, the IP address for **PC1** is incorrect as verified with the **ipconfig** command.

    c. Suggest a solution that you think will resolve the problem and document it. For example, change the IP address for **PC1** to match the documentation.

Note: Often, there is more than one solution. However, it is a troubleshooting best practice to implement and verify one solution at a time. Implementing more than one solution could introduce additional issues in a more complex scenario.

Part 2: Implement, Verify, and Document Solutions

In Part 2 of this activity, you will implement the solutions you identified in Part 1. You will then verify the solution worked. You may need to return to Part 1 to finish isolating all the problems.

Step 1: Implement solutions to connectivity problems.

Refer to your documentation in Part 1. Choose the first issue and implement your suggested solution. For example, correct the IP address on **PC1**.

Step 2: Verify that the problem is now resolved.

    a. Verify your solution has solved the problem by performing the test you used to identify the problem. For example, can **PC1** now ping **PC2**?

    b. If the problem is resolved, indicate so in your documentation. For example, in the Testing and Verification Documentation table above, a simple checkmark would suffice in the **Verified** column.

Step 3: Verify that all issues are resolved.

    a. If you still have an outstanding issue with a solution that has not yet been implemented, return to Part 2, Step 1.

    b. If all your current issues are resolved, have you also resolved any remote connectivity issues (such as can **PC1** ping **PC4**)? If the answer is no, return to Part 1, Step 1c to test remote connectivity.

29.2.6 Packet Tracer–Verify IPv4 and IPv6 Addressing

Addressing Table

Device	Interface	IP Address / Prefix		Default Gateway
R1	G0/0	10.10.1.97	255.255.255.224	N/A
		2001:db8:1:1::1/64		
	S0/0/1	10.10.1.6	255.255.255.252	N/A
		2001:db8:1:2::2/64		
		fe80::1		
R2	S0/0/0	10.10.1.5	255.255.255.252	N/A
		2001:db8:1:2::1/64		
	S0/0/1	10.10.1.9	255.255.255.252	N/A
		2001:db8:1:3::1/64		
		fe80::2		
R3	G0/0	10.10.1.17	255.255.255.240	N/A
		2001:db8:1:4::1/64		
R3	S0/0/1	10.10.1.10	255.255.255.252	N/A
		2001:db8:1:3::2/64		
		fe80::3		
PC1	NIC			
PC2	NIC			

Objectives

- Part 1: Complete the Addressing Table Documentation
- Part 2: Test Connectivity Using Ping
- Part 3: Discover the Path by Tracing the Route

Background / Scenario

Dual-stack allows IPv4 and IPv6 to coexist on the same network. In this activity, you will investigate a dual-stack implementation including documenting the IPv4 and IPv6 configuration for end devices, testing connectivity for both IPv4 and IPv6 using **ping** and end-to-end path tracing for IPv4 and IPv6.

Part 1: Complete the Addressing Table Documentation

Step 1: Use ipconfig to verify IPv4 addressing.

a.   Click **PC1** and open the **Command Prompt**.

b.   Enter the **ipconfig /all** command to collect the IPv4 information. Fill-in the Addressing Table with the IPv4 address, subnet mask, and default gateway.

c.   Click **PC2** and open the **Command Prompt**.

d.   Enter the **ipconfig /all** command to collect the IPv4 information. Fill-in the Addressing Table with the IPv4 address, subnet mask, and default gateway.

Step 2: Use ipv6config to verify IPv6 addressing.

a.   On **PC1**, enter the **ipv6config /all** command to collect the IPv6 information. Fill-in the **Addressing Table** with the IPv6 address, subnet prefix, and default gateway.

b.   On **PC2**, enter the **ipv6config /all** command to collect the IPv6 information. Fill-in the **Addressing Table** with the IPv6 address, subnet prefix, and default gateway.

Part 2: Test Connectivity Using Ping

Step 1: Use ping to verify IPv4 connectivity.

a.   From **PC1**, ping the IPv4 address for **PC2**.

Question:

Was the result successful?

_____

b.   From **PC2**, ping the IPv4 address for **PC1**.

Question:

Was the result successful?

_____

Step 2: Use ping to verify IPv6 connectivity.

a.   From **PC1**, ping the IPv6 address for **PC2**.

Question:

Was the result successful?

_____

b.   From **PC2**, ping the IPv6 address of **PC1**.

Question:

Was the result successful?

_____

Part 3: Discover the Path by Tracing the Route

Step 1: Use tracert to discover the IPv4 path.

    a. From **PC1**, trace the route to **PC2**.

```
PC> tracert 10.10.1.20
```

Questions:

What addresses were encountered along the path?

_____

With which interfaces are the four addresses associated

_____

    b. From **PC2**, trace the route to **PC1**.

Questions:

What addresses were encountered along the path?

_____

With which interfaces are the four addresses associated?

_____

Step 2: Use tracert to discover the IPv6 path.

    a. From **PC1**, trace the route to the IPv6 address for **PC2**.

```
PC> tracert 2001:db8:1:4::a
```

Questions:

What addresses were encountered along the path?

_____

With which interfaces are the four addresses associated?

_____

    b. From **PC2**, trace the route to the IPv6 address for **PC1**.

Questions:

What addresses were encountered along the path?

_____

With which interfaces are the four addresses associated?

_____

29.2.7 Packet Tracer–Use Ping and Traceroute to Test Network Connectivity

Addressing Table

Device	Interface	IP Address / Prefix		Default Gateway
R1	G0/0	2001:db8:1:1::1/64		N/A
	G0/1	10.10.1.97	255.255.255.224	N/A
	S0/0/1	10.10.1.6	255.255.255.252	N/A
	S0/0/1	2001:db8:1:2::2/64		
	S0/0/1	fe80::1		
R2	S0/0/0	10.10.1.5	255.255.255.252	N/A
	S0/0/0	2001:db8:1:2::1/64		
	S0/0/1	10.10.1.9	255.255.255.252	N/A
	S0/0/1	2001:db8:1:3::1/64		
	S0/0/1	fe80::2		
R3	G0/0	2001:db8:1:4::1/64		N/A
	G0/1	10.10.1.17	255.255.255.240	N/A
	S0/0/1	10.10.1.10	255.255.255.252	N/A
	S0/0/1	2001:db8:1:3::2/64		
	S0/0/1	fe80::3		
PC1	NIC			
PC2	NIC			
PC3	NIC			
PC4	NIC			

Objectives

- Part 1: Test and Restore IPv4 Connectivity
- Part 2: Test and Restore IPv6 Connectivity

Background / Scenario

There are connectivity issues in this activity. In addition to gathering and documenting information about the network, you will locate the problems and implement acceptable solutions to restore connectivity.

Note: The user EXEC password is **cisco**. The privileged EXEC password is **class**.

Instructions

Part 1: Test and Restore IPv4 Connectivity

Step 1: Use ipconfig and ping to verify connectivity.

   a. Click **PC1** and open the **Command Prompt**.

   b. Enter the **ipconfig /all** command to collect the IPv4 information. Complete the Addressing Table with the IPv4 address, subnet mask, and default gateway.

   c. Click **PC3** and open the **Command Prompt**.

   d. Enter the **ipconfig /all** command to collect the IPv4 information. Complete the Addressing Table with the IPv4 address, subnet mask, and default gateway.

   e. Use the **ping** command to test connectivity between **PC1** and **PC3**. The ping should fail.

Step 2: Locate the source of connectivity failure.

   a. From **PC1**, enter the necessary command to trace the route to **PC3**.

   Question:

   What is the last successful IPv4 address that was reached?

   _____

   b. The trace will eventually end after 30 attempts. Press **Ctrl+C** to stop the trace before 30 attempts.

   c. From **PC3**, enter the necessary command to trace the route to **PC1**.

   Question:

   What is the last successful IPv4 address that was reached?

   _____

   d. Press **Ctrl+C** to stop the trace.

   e. Click **R1**. Press **ENTER** and log in to the router.

   f. Enter the **show ip interface brief** command to list the interfaces and their status. There are two IPv4 addresses on the router. One should have been recorded in Step 2a.

   Question:

   What is the other?

   _____

   g. Enter the **show ip route** command to list the networks to which the router is connected. Note that there are two networks connected to the **Serial0/0/1** interface.

   Question:

   What are they?

   _____

h.   Repeat steps 2e through 2g with **R3** and record your answers.

_____

i.   Click **R2**. Press **Enter** and log into the router.

j.   Enter the **show ip interface brief** command and record your addresses.

_____

k.   Run more tests if it helps visualize the problem. Simulation mode is available.

Step 3: Propose a solution to solve the problem.

Compare your answers in step 2 to the documentation you have available for the network.

Question:

What is the error?

_____

What solution would you propose to correct the problem?

_____

Step 4: Implement the plan.

Implement the solution you proposed in step 3b.

Step 5: Verify that connectivity is restored.

a.   From **PC1** test connectivity to **PC3**.

b.   From **PC3** test connectivity to **PC1**.

Question:

Is the problem resolved?

_____

Step 6: Document the solution.

Part 2: Test and Restore IPv6 Connectivity

Step 1: Use ipv6config and ping to verify connectivity.

a.   Click **PC2** and open the **Command Prompt**.

b.   Enter the **ipv6config /all** command to collect the IPv6 information. Complete the Addressing Table with the IPv6 address, subnet prefix, and default gateway.

c.   Click **PC4** and open the **Command Prompt**.

d.   Enter the **ipv6config /all** command to collect the IPv6 information. Complete the Addressing Table with the IPv6 address, subnet prefix, and default gateway.

e.   Test connectivity between **PC2** and **PC4**. The ping should fail.

Step 2: Locate the source of connectivity failure.

a.   From **PC2**, enter the necessary command to trace the route to **PC4**.

Question:

What is the last successful IPv6 address that was reached?

_____

b. The trace will eventually end after 30 attempts. Enter **Ctrl+C** to stop the trace before 30 attempts.

c. From **PC4**, enter the necessary command to trace the route to **PC2**.

Question:

What is the last successful IPv6 address that was reached?

_____

d. Enter **Ctrl+C** to stop the trace.

e. Click **R3**. Press **Enter** and log in to the router.

f. Enter the **show ipv6 interface brief** command to list the interfaces and their status. There are two IPv6 addresses on the router. One should match the gateway address recorded in step 1d.

Question:

Is there a discrepancy?

_____

_____

g. Run more tests if it helps visualize the problem. The simulation mode is available.

Step 3: Propose a solution to solve the problem.

Compare your answers in step 2 to the documentation you have available for the network.

Question:

What is the error?

_____

What solution would you propose to correct the problem?

_____

Configure PC4 with the correct default gateway address: FE80::3.

Step 4: Implement the plan.

Implement the solution you proposed in step 3b.

Step 5: Verify that connectivity is restored.

a. From **PC2** test connectivity to **PC4**.

b. From **PC4** test connectivity to **PC2**.

Question:

Is the problem resolved?

_____

Step 6: Document the solution.

Packet Tracer
☐ Activity

29.3.1 Packet Tracer–Use ICMP to Test and Correct Network Connectivity

Addressing Table

Device	Interface	Address	Mask/Prefix	Default Gateway
RTR-1	G/0/0/0	192.168.1.1	255.255.255.0	N/A
		2001:db8:4::1	/64	N/A
	S0/1/0	10.10.2.2	255.255.255.252	N/A
		2001:db8:2::2	/126	N/A
	S0/1/1	10.10.3.1	255.255.255.252	N/A
		2001:db8:3::1	/126	N/A
RTR-2	G/0/0/0	10.10.1.1	255.255.255.0	N/A
	G0/0/1	2001:db8:1::1	/64	N/A
	S0/1/0	10.10.2.1	255.255.255.252	N/A
		2001:db8:2::1	/126	N/A
RTR-3	G0/0/0	10.10.5.1	255.255.255.0	N/A
	G0/0/1	2001:db8:5::1	/64	N/A
	S0/1/0	10.10.3.2	255.255.255.252	N/A
		2001:db8:3::2	/126	N/A
PC-1	NIC	10.10.1.10	255.255.255.0	10.10.1.1
Laptop A	NIC	10.10.1.20	255.255.255.0	10.10.1.1
PC-2	NIC	2001:db8:1::10	/64	fe80::1
PC-3	NIC	2001:db8:1::20	/64	fe80::1
PC-4	NIC	10.10.5.10	255.255.255.0	10.10.5.1
Server 1	NIC	10.10.5.20	255.255.255.0	10.10.5.1
Laptop B	NIC	2001:db8:5::10	/64	fe80::1
Laptop C	NIC	2001:db8:5::20	/64	fe80::1
Corporate Server	NIC	203.0.113.100	255.255.255.0	203.0.113.1
Corporate Server	NIC	2001:db8:acad::100	/64	fe80::1

Objectives

In this Packet Tracer activity, you will use ICMP to test network connectivity and locate network problems. You will also correct simple configuration issues and restore connectivity to the network.

- Use ICMP to locate connectivity issues.

- Configure network devices to correct connectivity issues.

Background / Scenario

Customers have been complaining that they can't reach some network resources. You have been asked to test connectivity in the network. You use ICMP to find out which resources are unreachable and the locations from which they can't be reached. Then, you use trace to locate the point at which network connectivity is broken. Finally, you fix the errors that you find to restore connectivity to the network.

Instructions

All hosts should have connectivity to all other hosts and the Corporate Server.

- Wait until all link lights are green.

- Select a host and use ICMP ping to determine which hosts are reachable from that host.

- If a host is found to be unreachable, use ICMP trace to locate the general location of the network errors.

- Locate the specific errors and correct them.

Physical Layer

This chapter contains no labs or packet tracers.

Data Link Layer

This chapter contains no labs or packet tracers.

Routing at the Network Layer

This chapter contains no labs or packet tracers.

33.4.6 Packet Tracer–Configure IPv6 Addressing

Addressing Table

Device	Interface	IPv6 Address/Prefix	Default Gateway
R1	G0/0	2001:db8:1:1::1/64	N/A
		fe80::1	
	G0/1	2001:db8:1:2::1/64	N/A
		fe80::1	
	S0/0/0	2001:db8:1:a001::2/64	N/A
		fe80::1	
Sales	NIC	2001:db8:1:1::2/64	fe80::1
Billing	NIC	2001:db8:1:1::3/64	fe80::1
Accounting	NIC	2001:db8:1:1::4/64	fe80::1
Design	NIC	2001:db8:1:2::2/64	fe80::1
Engineering	NIC	2001:db8:1:2::3/64	fe80::1
CAD	NIC	2001:db8:1:2::4/64	fe80::1
ISP	S0/0/0	2001:db8:1:a001::1	fe80::1

Objectives

- Part 1: Configure IPv6 Addressing on the Router
- Part 2: Configure IPv6 Addressing on Servers
- Part 3: Configure IPv6 Addressing on Clients
- Part 4: Test and Verify Network Connectivity

Background

In this activity, you will practice configuring IPv6 addresses on a router, servers, and clients. You will also practice verifying your IPv6 addressing implementation.

Part 1: Configure IPv6 Addressing on the Router

Step 1: Enable the router to forward IPv6 packets.

a. Click **R1** and then the CLI tab. Press **Enter**.

b. Enter privileged EXEC mode.

c. Enter the **ipv6 unicast-routing** global configuration command. This command must be entered to enable the router to forward IPv6 packets.

```
R1(config)# ipv6 unicast-routing
```

Step 2: Configure IPv6 addressing on GigabitEthernet0/0.

    a. Enter the commands necessary to move to interface configuration mode for GigabitEthernet0/0.

    b. Configure the **IPv6 Address** with the following command:

```
R1(config-if)# ipv6 address 2001:db8:1:1::1/64
```

    c. Configure the link-local **IPv6 Address** with the following command:

```
R1(config-if)# ipv6 address fe80::1 link-local
```

    d. Activate the interface.

```
R1(config-if)# no shutdown
```

Step 3: Configure IPv6 addressing on GigabitEthernet0/1.

    a. Enter the commands necessary to move to interface configuration mode for GigabitEthernet0/1.

    b. Refer to the Addressing Table for the correct IPv6 address.

    c. Configure the **IPv6 Address** and link-local address and activate the interface.

Step 4: Configure IPv6 addressing on Serial0/0/0.

    a. Enter the commands necessary to move to interface configuration mode for Serial0/0/0.

    b. Refer to the Addressing Table for the correct IPv6 address.

    c. Configure the **IPv6 Address** and link-local address and activate the interface.

Step 5: Verify IPv6 addressing on R1.

It is good practice to verify addressing when it is complete by comparing configured values with the values in the Addressing Table.

    a. Exit configuration mode on **R1**.

    b. Verify the addressing configured by issuing the following command:

```
R1# show ipv6 interface brief
```

    c. If any addresses are incorrect, repeat the steps above as necessary to make any corrections.

Note: To make a change in addressing with IPv6, you must remove the incorrect address, or both the correct address and incorrect address will remain configured on the interface.

Example:

```
R1(config-if)# no ipv6 address 2001:db8:1:5::1/64
```

    d. Save the router configuration to NVRAM.

Part 2: Configure IPv6 Addressing on the Servers

Step 1: Configure IPv6 addressing on the Accounting Server.

    a. Click **Accounting** and click the **Desktop** tab and select **IP Configuration**.

    b. Set the **IPv6 Address** to **2001:db8:1:1::4** with a prefix of **/64**.

    c. Set the **IPv6 Gateway** to the link-local address, **fe80::1**.

Step 2: Configure IPv6 addressing on the CAD Server.

Configure the **CAD** server with addresses as was done in step 1. Refer to the Addressing Table for the addresses to use.

Part 3: Configure IPv6 Addressing on the Clients

Step 1: Configure IPv6 addressing on the Sales and Billing Clients.

a. Click **Billing** and then select the **Desktop** tab followed by **IP Configuration**.

b. Set the **IPv6 Address** to **2001:db8:1:1::3** with a prefix of **/64**.

c. Set the **IPv6 Gateway** to the link-local address, **fe80::1**.

d. Repeat steps 1a through 1c for **Sales**. Refer to the Addressing Table for the **IPv6 Address**.

Step 2: Configure IPv6 Addressing on the Engineering and Design Clients.

a. Click **Engineering**, select the **Desktop** tab, and choose **IP Configuration**.

b. Set the **IPv6 Address** to 2001:db8:1:2::3 with a prefix of **/64**.

c. Set the **IPv6 Gateway** to the link-local address, **fe80::1**.

d. Repeat steps 2a through 2c for **Design**. Refer to the Addressing Table for the **IPv6 Address**.

Part 4: Test and Verify Network Connectivity

Step 1: Open the server web pages from the clients.

a. Click **Sales**, followed by the **Desktop** tab. Close the **IP Configuration** window if necessary.

b. Click **Web Browser**. Enter **2001:db8:1:1::4** in the URL box and click **Go**. The **Accounting** website should appear.

c. Enter **2001:db8:1:2::4** in the URL box and click **Go**. The **CAD** website should appear.

d. Repeat steps 1a through 1c for the rest of the clients.

Step 2: Ping the ISP.

a. Click any client.

b. Click the Desktop tab and choose **Command Prompt**.

c. Test connectivity to the ISP by entering the following command:

```
PC> ping 2001:db8:1:a001::1
```

d. Repeat the **ping** command with other clients until full connectivity is verified.

33.5.4 Lab–Identify IPv6 Addresses

Objectives

- Part 1: Practice with Different Types of IPv6 Addresses
- Part 2: Examine a Host IPv6 Network Interface and Address

Background / Scenario

With the depletion of the Internet Protocol version 4 (IPv4) network address space and the adoption and transition to IPv6, networking professionals must understand how both IPv4 and IPv6 networks function. Many devices and applications already support IPv6. This includes extensive Cisco device Internetwork Operating System (IOS) support and workstation/server operating system support, such as that found in Windows and Linux.

This lab focuses on IPv6 addresses and the components of the address. In Part 1, you will identify the IPv6 address types and IPv6 addresses abbreviation. In Part 2, you will view the IPv6 settings on a PC.

Required Resources

- 1 PC (Windows with internet access)

Instructions

Part 1: Practice with Different Types of IPv6 Addresses

In this part, you will identify the different types of IPv6 Addresses and practice compressing and decompressing IPv6 addresses.

Step 1: Match the IPv6 address to its type.

Match the IPv6 addresses to their corresponding address type. Notice that the addresses have been compressed to their abbreviated notation and the slash network prefix number is not shown. Some answer choices must be used more than once.

Answer choices:

a. Loopback address

b. Global unicast address

c. Link-local address

d. Unique-local address

e. Multicast address

IPv6 Address	Answer
2001:0db8:1:acad::fe55:6789:b210	B
::1	A
fc00:22:a:2::cd4:23e4:76fa	D
2033:db8:1:1:22:a33d:259a:21fe	B

IPv6 Address	Answer
fe80::3201:cc01:65b1	C
ff00::	E
ff00::db7:4322:a231:67c	E
ff02::2	E

Step 2: Practice compressing and decompressing IPv6 addresses.

Questions:

Using the rules of IPv6 address abbreviation, either compress or decompress the following addresses:

2002:0ec0:0200:0001:0000:04eb:44ce:08a2

_____

_____

_____

_____

_____

Part 2: Examine a Host IPv6 Network Interface and Address

In Part 2, you will check the IPv6 network settings of your PC to identify your network interface IPv6 address.

Step 1: Check your PC IPv6 network address settings.

Verify that the IPv6 protocol is installed and active on your PC-A. (Check your Local Area Connection settings.)

a. Navigate to the **Control Panel**.

b. In the Category View, click the **Network and Sharing Center** icon. Click **View network status and tasks**.

c. In the Network and Sharing Center window, you will see your active networks.

d. On the left side of the window, click **Change adapter settings.** You should now see icons representing your installed network adapters. Right-click your active network interface (it may be an **Ethernet** or **Wi-Fi**), and then click **Properties.**

e. In the Properties window, scroll through the list of items to determine whether IPv6 is present, which indicates that it is installed, and if checkmarked, which indicates that it is active.

f. Select the item **Internet Protocol Version 6 (TCP/IPv6)** and click **Properties.** You should see the IPv6 settings for your network interface. Your IPv6 properties window is likely set to **Obtain an IPv6 address automatically**. This does not mean that IPv6 relies on the Dynamic Host Configuration Protocol (DHCP). Instead of using DHCP, IPv6 looks to the local router for IPv6 network information and then auto-configures its own IPv6 addresses. To manually configure IPv6, you must provide the IPv6 address, the subnet prefix length, and the default gateway. Click **Cancel** to exit the properties windows.

Note: The local router can refer host requests for IPv6 information, especially Domain Name System (DNS) information, to a DHCPv6 server on the network.

g. After you have verified that IPv6 is installed and active on your PC, you should check your IPv6 address information.

Step 2: Verify the IPv6 address settings using the Command Prompt.

a. Open a command prompt and enter the **ipconfig /all** command. Your output should look similar to this:

```
C:\Users\user> ipconfig /all


Windows IP Configuration


<output omitted>


Wireless LAN adapter Wireless Network Connection:

    Connection-specific DNS Suffix  . :
    Description . . . . . . . . . . . : Intel(R) Centrino(R) Advanced-N
6200 AGN
    Physical Address. . . . . . . . . : 02-37-10-41-FB-48
    DHCP Enabled. . . . . . . . . . . : Yes
    Autoconfiguration Enabled . . . . : Yes
    Link-local IPv6 Address . . . . . : fe80::8d4f:4f4d:3237:95e2%14
(Preferred)
    IPv4 Address. . . . . . . . . . . : 192.168.2.106(Preferred)
    Subnet Mask . . . . . . . . . . . : 255.255.255.0
    Lease Obtained. . . . . . . . . . : Sunday, January 06, 2013 9:47:36 AM
    Lease Expires . . . . . . . . . . : Monday, January 07, 2013 9:47:38 AM
        Default Gateway . . . . . . . . : 192.168.2.1
        DHCP Server . . . . . . . . . . : 192.168.2.1
        DHCPv6 IAID . . . . . . . . . . : 335554320
        DHCPv6 Client DUID. . . . . . . :
    00-01-00-01-14-57-84-B1-1C-C1-DE-91-C3-5D

        DNS Servers . . . . . . . . . . : 192.168.1.1
                                          8.8.4.4
        <output omitted>
```

b. You can see from the output that the client PC has an IPv6 link-local address with a randomly generated interface ID.

Questions:

What does it indicate about the network regarding IPv6 global unicast address, IPv6 unique-local address, or IPv6 gateway address?

_____

_____

What kind of IPv6 addresses did you find when using **ipconfig /all**?

_____

_____

Reflection Questions

1. How do you think you must support IPv6 in the future?

2. Do you think IPv4 networks continue on, or will everyone eventually switch over to IPv6? How long do you think it will take?

CHAPTER 34

IPv6 Neighbor Discovery

Packet Tracer
☐ Activity

34.1.4 Packet Tracer–IPv6 Neighbor Discovery

Addressing Table

Device	Interface	IPv6 Address / Prefix	Default Gateway
RTA	G0/0/0	2001:db8:acad:1::1/64	N/A
RTA	G0/0/1	2001:db8:acad:1::1/64	N/A
PCA1	NIC	2001:db8:acad:1::a/64	fe80::1
PCA2	NIC	2001:db8:acad:1::b/64	fe80::1
PCB1	NIC	2001:db8:acad:2::a/64	fe80::1

Objectives

- Part 1: IPv6 Neighbor Discovery Local Network
- Part 2: IPv6 Neighbor Discovery Remote Network

Background

For a device to communicate with another device, the MAC address of the destination must be known. With IPv6, a process called Neighbor Discovery using the NDP or ND protocol is responsible for determining the destination MAC address. You will gather PDU information in **Simulation Mode** to better understand the process. There is no Packet Tracer scoring for this activity.

Instructions

Part 1: IPv6 Neighbor Discovery Local Network

In this part, you will obtain the MAC address of a destination device on the same network.

Step 1: Check the router for any neighbors that it discovered.

a. Click the **RTA Router**. Select the **CLI** tab and issue the command **show ipv6 neighbors** from the privileged EXEC mode. If there are any entries displayed, remove them using the **clear ipv6 neighbors** command.

b. Click **PCA1**, select the **Desktop** tab, and click the **Command Prompt** icon.

Step 2: Switch to Simulation Mode to capture events.

a. Click the **Simulation** button in the lower right corner of the Packet Tracer Topology window.

b. Click the **Show All/None** button in the **Simulation Panel** until **Event List Filters – Visible Events** displays **None**.

c. Click **Edit Filters**. Select the IPv6 tab at the top and check the boxes for **ICMPv6** and **NDP**. Close the Edit **ACL Filters** window. Now the Event List Filters displays ICMPv6 and NDP.

    d. From the command prompt on **PCA1**, issue the command **ping −n 1 2001:db8:acad:1::b**. This will start the process of pinging **PCA2**.

    e. Click **Play (Hands Free)** in the **Play Controls** outside the **Simulation Panel**. If prompted, click **View Previous Events** in the **Buffer Full - Packet Tracer** window. You should have approximately 12 entries in the window.

        Question:

        Why are ND PDUs present?

        _____

    f. Click the square in the **Type** column for the first event, which should be **ICMPv6**.

        Question:

        Because the message starts with this event, there is only an Outbound PDU, so on the **OSI Model** tab, what is the **Message Type** listed for **ICMPv6**?

        _____

        Notice there is no Layer 2 addressing. Click the **Next Layer >>** button to get an explanation about the ND (Neighbor Discovery) process.

    g. Click the square for the next event in the **Simulation Panel**. It should be at device **PCA1**, and the type should be **NDP**.

        Questions:

        What changed in the Layer 3 addressing?

        _____

        What Layer 2 addresses are shown?

        _____

        When a host does not know the destination's MAC address, a special multicast MAC address is used by IPv6 Neighbor Discovery as the Layer 2 destination address.

    h. Navigate back to the **Event List**. Select the first **NDP** event at SwitchA.

        Question:

        Is there any difference between the **In Layers** and **Out Layers** for **Layer 2**?

        _____

    i. Select the first **NDP** event at PCA2. Click **Outbound PDU Details**.

        Question:

        What addresses are displayed for the following?

        Ethernet II DEST ADDR:

        _____

        Ethernet II SRC ADDR:

        _____

        IPv6 SRC IP:

        _____

IPv6 DST IP:

_____

_____

Note: The addresses in the fields may be wrapped, adjust the size of the PDU window to make address information easier to read.

Question:

j. Select the first **NDP** event at **RTA**. Why are there no **Out Layers?**

_____

k. Click through the **Next Layer >>** button until the end and read steps 4 through 7 for further explanation.

l. Click the next **ICMPv6** event at **PCA1**.

Question:

Does **PCA1** now have all the necessary information to communicate with **PCA2?**

_____

m. Click the last **ICMPv6** event at **PCA1**. Notice this is the last communication listed.

Question:

What is the **ICMPv6 Echo Message Type?**

_____

n. Click the **Reset Simulation** button in the **Simulation Panel**. From the command prompt of **PCA1**, repeat the **ping** to **PCA2**. (Hint: you should be able to press the up arrow to bring the previous command back.)

o. Click **Play (Hands Free)** to complete the ping process. Click **View Previous Events** if prompted.

Question:

Why were there no NDP events?

_____

Part 2: IPv6 Neighbor Discovery Remote Network

In Part 2 of this activity, you will perform steps similar to those in the previous part, except in this case, the destination host is on another LAN. Observe how the Neighbor Discovery process differs from the process you observed in the previous part. Pay close attention to some of the additional addressing steps that take place when a device communicates with a device that is on a different network.

Step 1: Capture events for remote communication.

a. Click the **Reset Simulation** button to clear out the previous events. Display and clear any entries in the IPv6 neighbor device table, as was done in the previous part.

b. Verify only **ICMPv6** and **NDP** are listed in **Event List Filters - Visible Events.**

c. From the command prompt on **PCA1**, issue the **ping –n 1 2001:db8:acad:2::a** command to ping host **PCB1**.

d. Click **Play (Hands Free)** in the **Play Controls** outside the **Simulation Panel**. If prompted, click **View Previous Events** in the **Buffer Full–Packet Tracer window**.

e. When the pinging process is done, click the square in the **Type** column for the first event, which should be **ICMPv6**. Because the message starts with this event, there is only an **Outbound PDU**. Notice that it is missing the Layer 2 information, as it did in the previous scenario.

f. Click the first **NDP** event At Device **PCA1**.

Question:

What address is being used for the Src IP in the **Inbound PDU**?

_____

IPv6 Neighbor Discovery will determine the next destination to forward the ICMPv6 message.

g. Click the second ICMPv6 event for **PCA1**. **PCA1** now has enough information to create an ICMPv6 echo request.

Question:

What MAC address is being used for the destination MAC?

_____

h. Click the next ICMPv6 event at device **RTA**. Notice that the **Outbound PDU** from RTA lacks the destination Layer 2 address, This means RTA once again has to perform a Neighbor Discovery for the interface with the 2001:db8:acad:2:: network because it does not know the MAC addresses of the devices on the G0/0/1 LAN.

i. Skip down to the first ICMPv6 event for device **PCB1**.

Question:

What is missing in the outbound Layer 2 information?

_____

j. The next few **NDP** events are associating the remaining IPv6 addresses to MAC addresses. The previous NDP events associated MAC addresses with Link Local addresses.

k. Skip to the last set of ICMPv6 events and notice that all the addresses have been learned. The required information is now known, so **PCB1** can send echo reply messages to **PCA1**.

l. Click the **Reset Simulation** button in the **Simulation Panel**. From the **PCA1** command prompt, repeat the command to ping **PCB1**.

m. Click **Play (Hands Free)** to complete the ping process. Click **View Previous Events** if prompted in the **Buffer Full** window.

Question:

Were there any NDP events?

_____

n. Click the only **PCB1** event in the new list.

Questions:

What does the destination MAC address correspond to?

_____

Why is **PCB1** using the router interface MAC address to make its ICMP PDUs?

_____

Step 2: Examine router outputs.

a. Return to **Realtime** mode.

b. Click **RTA** and select the **CLI** tab. At the router prompt enter the command **show ipv6 neighbors.**

Questions:

How many addresses are listed?

_____

What devices are these addresses associated with?

_____

Are there any entries for PCA2 listed? Explain.

_____

c. Ping **PCA2** from the router.

d. Issue the **show ipv6 neighbors** command.

Question:

Are there entries for **PCA2**?

_____

Reflection Questions

1. When does a device require the IPv6 Neighbor Discovery process?

_____

2. How does a router help minimize the amount of IPv6 Neighbor Discovery traffic on a network?

_____

3. How does IPv6 minimize the impact of the ND process on network hosts?

_____

4. How does the Neighbor Discovery process differ when a destination host is on the same LAN or a remote LAN?

_____

Cisco Switches and Routers

This chapter contains no labs or packet tracers.

Troubleshoot Common Network Problems

 ## 36.4.10 Lab–Troubleshoot Using Network Utilities

Objectives

- Interpret the output of commonly used network command-line utilities.
- Determine which network utility can provide the necessary information to perform troubleshooting activities in a bottom-up troubleshooting strategy.

Background/Scenario

There are a number of problems that can cause networking connectivity issues. In this lab, you will use network utilities that can help you to identify connectivity issues in wireless networks. The network command-line utilities are also useful to detect problems in a wired network.

Required Resources

- One PC (Windows 10 with a wired and wireless NIC installed)
- A wireless router
- Internet connectivity

Instructions

Part 1: Network Connections

Step 1: Connect to a wireless network.

    a. Disconnect the Ethernet cable from your computer. An "orange triangle" appears over the **Connections** icon in the system tray.

    b. Click the **Connection** icon in the system tray.

    Question:

    What is the name of an available wireless connection?

    _____

    c. Click one of the available wireless connections. Connect to the network. Enter log-in information if required.

    d. Confirm that the connection is successful.

Step 2: Verify that the network adapter is operational.

    When a connectivity problem is reported, the first step in a bottom-up troubleshooting strategy is to determine whether the NIC and the operating system settings on the computer are functioning correctly.

    a. Right-click **Start** and select **Control Panel**. Click **Network and Sharing Center** and choose **Change adapter settings**.

b. Select the **Wireless Network Connection**. Right click the adapter and select **Status** from the menu. If the **Status** choice is grayed out, the adapter is either not enabled or not connected to a wireless SSID.

c. In the Status window, verify that the connection is enabled and that the connection SSID is correct. Click **Details** to open the Adapter Details window.

d. The Details window shows the current IP configuration active on the network adapter. It displays both the IPv4 and IPv6 configurations. If DHCP is active, the lease information is shown.

Questions:

Is DHCP enabled on the PC?

_____

When does the DHCP lease expire?

_____

Step 3: Confirm correct network configuration.

a. Open a command prompt.

b. Enter **ping 127.0.0.1**. The IP address 127.0.0.1 is also referred to as the localhost address. A successful ping to the localhost address indicates that the TCP/IP protocol stack is operational on the computer. If the localhost address does not reply to a **ping** command, there might be an issue with the device driver or the network interface card.

Question:

Was the **ping** command successful?

_____

c. Use the **ipconfig** command. Identify the IP address, subnet mask, and default gateway addresses configured on the computer.

If the local IPv4 address is a host address on the 169.254.0.0/16 network, the computer received its IP address configuration through the Automatic Private IP Addressing (APIPA) feature of the Windows operating system.

Question:

What problems can cause a computer to receive an APIPA address?

_____

If the computer is assigned an APIPA address, there might be an issue with the DHCP server. If the wireless router is providing the DHCP services, confirm that the DHCP service is configured correctly and that the IP address range is large enough to accommodate all the devices that may attach wirelessly.

Question:

What is the IP address of the default gateway assigned to your PC?

_____

d. To test if the PC can reach the default gateway through the network, **ping** the default gateway IP address.

A successful **ping** indicates that there is a connection between the computer and the default gateway.

If the **ping** command does not complete successfully, make sure that the IP address of the gateway is typed correctly, and that the wireless connection is active.

e. Type **net view**. When issued on a Windows PC, the **net view** command displays the computer names of other Windows devices in your Windows domain or workgroup. When **net view** displays the names of other computers, your computer can successfully send messages across the network.

```
C:\Users\Student> net view
```

Question:

List the computer names displayed.

_____

_____

Note: Depending on the configuration of the PCs in your lab, **net view** may not return any computer names or may display an error message. If either happen, move on to the next part.

Part 2: External Connectivity

Step 1: Test external connectivity.

If you have an external connection, use the following methods to verify the operation of the default gateway and DNS service.

Note: Your output may vary.

a. The Windows **tracert** command performs the same function as the **traceroute** command used in the Cisco IOS. Use the **tracert** command, along with the URL for your school's website or the Cisco Networking Academy website. For example, enter **tracert www.netacad.com**.

```
C:\Users\Student> tracert www.netacad.com

Tracing route to Liferay-Prod-1009279580.us.-east-1.elb.amazonaws.com
[52.5.233.103]

over a maximum of 30 hops:
    1     1 ms    57 ms     3 ms   192.168.1.1
    2     *        12 ms    12 ms   10.39.176.1
    3    14 ms    28 ms    11 ms   100.127.65.248
    4    10 ms    26 ms    21 ms   70.169.73.90
    5    35 ms    32 ms    36 ms   68.1.2.109
<output omitted>
Trace complete.
```

The **tracert** command displays the path taken by the packet between the source and destination IP addresses. Each router the packet travels through to reach the destination address is shown as a hop in the **tracert** output. If a network issue occurs on the path, the **tracert** output will stop after the last successful hop. The first hop in the output is the default gateway of the source PC, and the last entry will be the destination address when the **tracert** command completes successfully.

b. The **tracert** command uses the configured DNS server to resolve the fully qualified domain name to an IP address before beginning to trace the router to the destination. Using **tracert** or **ping** with a domain name instead of an IP address can confirm that the DNS server is providing name resolution services.

Questions:

What IP address was returned by the DNS server?

_____

What would happen if the DNS server could not resolve the domain name of the server?

_____

c. Use the **nslookup** command with the IP address you just discovered. The **nslookup** command is a utility that can be used to troubleshoot DNS problems.

Type **nslookup 72.163.6.233**. The IP address in this example is assigned to a server at Cisco Systems.

Questions:

What domain name was returned?

_____

What DNS server did the **nslookup** command use to resolve the domain name?

_____

Does the DNS server IP address match the one displayed in the **ipconfig /all** output?

_____

d. When the configured DNS server cannot resolve domain names or IP addresses, it is possible to set **nslookup** to try to resolve the names using a different DNS server. If another DNS server can resolve the addresses, but the configured DNS server cannot, there could be a problem with the DNS server configuration. Enter **nslookup /?** to view the options that can be used to test and troubleshoot DNS issues.

```
C:\Users\Student> nslookup /?
Usage:
    nslookup [-opt ...]             # interactive mode using default server
    nslookup [-opt ...] - server    # interactive mode using 'server'
    nslookup [-opt ...] host         # just look up 'host' using default server
    nslookup [-opt ...] host server # just look up 'host' using 'server'
```

Step 2: Test Application layer connectivity.

Open a web browser. Enter **www.cisco.com** in the **Address** field.

Question:

Does the **cisco.com** web page load in the browser? What underlying network functions have to be working for the web page load?

_____

Reflection Questions

1. The steps in this lab represent a bottom-up troubleshooting strategy, where the effort starts with the OSI model Physical layer and finishes with verifying the functionality of the Application layer. What are the other two troubleshooting strategies used by network technicians to isolate problems?

    _____

2. Which strategy would try first when presented with a network connectivity problem? Explain.

    _____

37.2.7 Packet Tracer–Connect a Network Based on a Network Diagram

Objectives

■ In this activity, you will complete a physical topology based on the provided network diagram.

Figure 37-1   Network Diagram

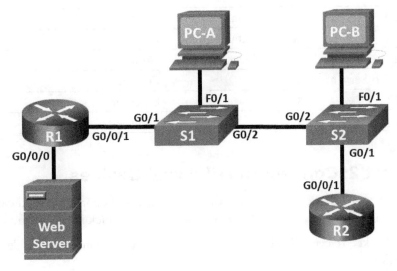

Instructions

Network diagrams are essential to visualizing how devices are connected and work together. Diagrams can act as road maps when troubleshooting and maintaining the network.

There are two types of network diagrams: logical and physical. A logical network diagram shows how the devices communicate with each other and the data flows through the network. A physical network diagram is similar to a floorplan. It shows all of the physical arrangements of the network, such as cable types, ports, server racks, and servers.

Part 1: Review the Logical Network Diagram

Review the above network diagram and record how the devices are connected in the Device table below:

Device Table

Device Name	Device Type	Local Interface	Connected Device and Port
R1	Router / Cisco 4321	G0/0/0	
R1	Router / Cisco 4321	G0/0/1	
S1	Switch / Catalyst 2960	G0/1	
S1	Switch / Catalyst 2960	G0/2	
S1	Switch / Catalyst 2960	F0/1	
S2	Switch / Catalyst 2960	G0/1	
S2	Switch / Catalyst 2960	G0/2	
S2	Switch / Catalyst 2960	F0/1	
R2	Router / Cisco 4321	G0/0/1	
Web Server	Server	Ethernet	
PC-A	PC	Ethernet	
PC-B	PC	Ethernet	

Part 2: Connect the Physical Devices

Now you have determined how the devices are interconnected, you can use information from the network diagram to connect the devices in the rack in the wiring closet.

In Packet Tracer's **Physical** mode, you can practice connecting the devices in the wiring closet rack.

Step 1: Determine the cable type.

From the network diagram, you have determined the devices are connected via Ethernet cables.

There are a few types of cables on the cable peg board in the main wiring closet.

Question:

What color are the straight-through Ethernet cables in Packet Tracer?

_____

Step 2: Connect the devices.

Using the Ethernet cables, connect the devices in the wiring closet according to the network diagram.

a. To connect router R1 to the Web Server, select an Ethernet cable from the peg board. The Web Server is the large device at the bottom of the equipment rack.

b. Click the Web Server's FastEthernet0 port to connect the Ethernet cable.

c. Click the GigabitEthernet0/0/1 on R1 to complete the connection. You can zoom into the device by right-clicking the device and selecting **Inspect Front**. Click the magnifying glass to zoom in on the front of the device. You can verify that the connection is up when the port LED lights blink green.

d. Repeat the procedure for all of the other connections to complete connecting the network. Note the PCs are located on the Addressing Table.

37.2.12 Packet Tracer–Use CDP to Map a Network

Addressing Table

Device	Interface	IP Address	Subnet Mask	Local Interface and Connected Neighbor
Edge1	G0/0	192.168.1.1	255.255.255.0	G0/1 - S1
	S0/0/0			S0/0/0 - ISP
	S0/0/1	209.165.200.10		S0/0/1 - ISP

Objectives

- Map a network using CDP and SSH remote access.

Background / Scenario

A senior network administrator requires you to map the Remote Branch Office network and discover the name of a recently installed switch that still needs an IP address to be configured. Your task is to create a map of the branch office network. You must record all the network device names, IP addresses, subnet masks, and physical interfaces interconnecting the network devices, as well as the name of the switch that does not have an IP address.

To map the network, you will use SSH for remote access and the Cisco Discovery Protocol (CDP) to discover information about neighboring network devices. Because CDP is a Layer 2 protocol, it can be used to discover information about devices that do not have IP addresses. You will record the gathered information to complete the Addressing Table and provide a topology diagram of the Remote Branch Office network.

The local and remote administrative usernames and passwords are:

Local Network

Username: **admin01**
Password: **S3cre7P@55**

Branch Office Network

    Username: **branchadmin**
    Password: **S3cre7P@55**

Instructions

Part 1: Use SSH to Remotely Access Network Devices

In Part 1, use the Admin-PC to remotely access the Edge1 gateway router. Next, from the Edge1 router, you will SSH into the Remote Branch Office.

  a. On the Admin-PC, open a command prompt.

  b. SSH into the gateway router at 192.168.1.1 using the username **admin01** and the password **S3cre7P@55**.

```
PC> ssh -1 admin01 192.168.1.1

Open

Password:

Edge1#
```

Note: Notice you are placed directly into privileged EXEC mode because the admin01 user account is set to privilege level 15.

---

  c. Use the **show ip interface brief** and **show interfaces** commands to document the Edge1 router's physical interfaces, IP addresses, and subnet masks in the Addressing Table.

  d. From Edge1, use SSH to access the Remote Branch Office at 209.165.200.10 with the username **branchadmin** and the same password as above:

```
Edge1# ssh -1 branchadmin 209.165.200.10

Open

Password:

Branch-Edge#
```

Question:

After connecting to the Remote Branch Office, what piece of previously missing information can now be added to the Addressing Table above?

Part 2: Use CDP to Discover Neighboring Devices

You are now remotely connected to the Branch-Edge router. Using CDP, begin looking for connected network devices.

  a. Issue the **show ip interface brief** and **show interfaces** commands to document the Branch-Edge router's network interfaces, IP addresses, and subnet masks. Add the missing information to the Addressing Table to map the network:

```
Branch-Edge# show ip interface brief
Branch-Edge# show interfaces
```

b. Security best practice recommends only running CDP when needed, so CDP might need turned on. Use the **show cdp** command to display its status.

```
Branch-Edge# show cdp

% CDP is not enabled
```

c. You need to turn on CDP, but it is a good idea to only broadcast CDP information to internal network devices, not to external networks. To do this, turn on the CDP protocol and disable CDP on the S0/0/1 interface.

```
Branch-Edge# configure terminal

Branch-Edge(config)# cdp run

Branch-Edge(config)# interface s0/0/1

Branch-Edge(config-if)# no cdp enable

Branch-Edge(config-if)# exit
```

d. Issue a **show cdp neighbors** command to find any neighboring network devices.

Note: CDP will only show connected Cisco devices that are also running CDP.

```
Branch-Edge# show cdp neighbors
```

Question:

Is there a neighboring network device? What type of device is it? What is its name? On what interface is it connected? Is the device's IP address listed? Record the information in the Addressing Table.

Note: It may take some time for CDP updates to be received. If you see no output from the command, press the **Fast Forward Time** button several times.

---

e. To find the IP address of the neighboring device, use the **show cdp neighbors detail** command and record the IP address:

```
Branch-Edge# show cdp neighbors detail
```

Question:

Aside from the neighboring device's IP address, what other piece of potentially sensitive information is listed?

---

f. Now that you know the IP address of the neighbor device, connect to it with SSH to discover other devices that may be its neighbors.

Note: To connect with SSH use the same Remote Branch Office username and password.

```
Branch-Edge# ssh -l branchadmin <the ip address of the neighbor device>
```

Questions:

What is the IP address of the neighbor device?

After successfully connecting with SSH, what does the command prompt show?

---

g. You are remotely connected to the next neighbor. Use the **show cdp neighbors** and **show cdp neighbors detail** commands to discover other connected neighbor devices.

Question:

What types of network devices neighbor this device? Record any newly discovered devices in the Addressing Table, including their hostnames, interfaces, and IP addresses.

h. Continue discovering new network devices using SSH and the **show CDP** commands. Eventually, you will reach the end of the network, and there will be no more devices to discover.

Question:

What is the name of the switch that does not have an IP address on the network?

i. Draw a topology of the Remote Branch Office network using the information you have gathered using CDP.

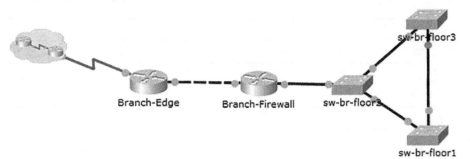

37.2.13 Packet Tracer–Troubleshooting Challenge –Document the Network

Addressing Table

Device	Interface	Device Type (router, switch, host)	IP Address	Subnet Mask	Default Gateway
PC1	NIC	Host			
PC2					
PC3					
PC4					
PC5					
PC6					
PC7					

Objectives

In this lab, you will document a network that is unknown to you.

- Test network connectivity
- Compile host addressing information
- Remotely access default gateway devices
- Document default gateway device configurations
- Discover devices on the network
- Draw the network topology

Background / Scenario

Your employer has been hired to take over the administration of a corporate network because the previous network administrator has left the company. The network documentation is missing and needs to be re-created. Your job is to document the hosts and network devices, including all the device addressing and logical interconnections. You will remotely access network devices, use network discovery to complete a device table, and draw the network topology.

This is part one of a two-part series of activities. You will use the documentation that you create in this activity to guide you as you troubleshoot the network in **Packet Tracer–Troubleshooting Challenge–Using Documentation to Solve Issues.**

As you investigate and document the network topology, make note of issues that you discover that do not adhere to the practices taught in the curriculum.

Instructions

Part 1: Test Connectivity

Ping between the PCs and the internet server to test the network. All PCs should be able to ping one another and the internet server.

Part 2: Discover PC Configuration Information

Go to the command prompt of each PC and display the IP settings. Record this information in the Addressing Table.

Part 3: Discover Information about the Default Gateway Devices

Connect to each default gateway device using the Telnet protocol and record information about the interfaces used in the table. The VTY password is **cisco**, and the privileged EXEC password is **class.**

```
C:\> telnet IP_address
```

Part 4: Reconstruct the Network Topology

In this part of the activity, you will continue recording information about the devices in the network in the Addressing Table. In addition, you will start to diagram the network topology based on what you can discover about the device interconnections.

Step 1: Access routing tables on each gateway device.

Use the routing tables in each router to learn more about the network. Make notes of your findings using the **show ip route** command.

Step 2: Discover non-gateway devices.

Use a network discovery protocol to display information about neighboring devices. Record your findings in the Addressing Table. At this point, you should also be able to begin documenting device interconnections.

Part 5: Further Explore Device Configurations and Interconnections

Step 1: Access device configurations.

Connect to the other devices on the network. Gather information about the device configurations using the **show running-config** command. Enter information for the active interfaces on each device.

Step 2: View neighbor information.

Use discovery protocols to increase your knowledge of the network devices and topologies.

Step 3: Connect to other devices.

Display configuration information for the other devices on the network. Record your findings in the Addressing Table.

By now, you should know about all the devices and interface configurations in the network. All rows of the table should contain device information. Use your information to reconstruct as much of the network topology as you can.

Step 4: Save your findings.

Be sure to save your completed documentation to be used in a later PT activity.

Reflection Questions

Which tools or commands did you find most useful for documenting the network?

_____

Security is a concern in this network. What two measures can be taken to make the network more secure?

_____

You may have noticed that some of the practices used to configure the network devices are out-of-date, inefficient, or not secure. Make a list of as recommendations regarding how the devices should be reconfigured to follow the best practices. Perform an internet search for recommendations if desired.

List your recommendations below:

37.4.9 Lab–Verify Address with a Subnet Calculator

Objectives

Subnet calculators can be helpful in providing information about a specific network or subnet. Typically, a subnet calculator will ask for a specific IPv4 or IPv6 address along with its subnet mask or prefix length. It will then calculate the address ranges for the full range of subnetworks specified.

In this activity, you will determine your device's IPv4 address and subnet mask and use an online subnet calculator to determine the IPv4 network address.

Instructions

Part 1: Determine Your Device's IPv4 Address and Subnet Mask

Depending on your device's operating system (computer or mobile phone), use the proper command to determine the following:

- IPv4 address
- Subnet mask

  Questions:

  What is IPv4 address and subnet mask for your device?

  _____

Part 2: Search for an Online Subnet Calculator

a. Using your web browser, search for **IP subnet calculator** to get a list of IP subnet calculators.

b. Choose an IP subnet calculator from the web search results.

Part 3: Enter the IPv4 Address and Subnet Mask

In the appropriate area, enter your device's IPv4 address and subnet mask. Perform the calculation to determine the IPv4 network address.

Part 4: Examine the IPv4 Network Address

The actual information provided will vary, but the most common information includes:

- Network address
- Range of host addresses
- Broadcast address
- Number of usable hosts

The IPv4 network address displayed is your device's network address. If the output includes a range of host addresses, your device's addresses should be within that range.

This information can be useful in verifying:

- If the device in question is on the same network as its default gateway.

- If two devices are on different networks, and therefore, proper routing must be utilized for reachability.

Note: Many of these subnet calculators will also give the address class: Class A, B or C. It is important to note that this information is no longer relevant. Classful addressing was discontinued with the introduction of Classless Inter-Domain Routing (CIDR) in 1993.

Using the information from the results, answer the following questions:

Questions:

What is your network address?

What is the range of host addresses?

What is the broadcast address?

What is the number of usable hosts?

37.5.3 Lab—Install Wireshark

Objectives

- Download and install Wireshark

Background / Scenario

Wireshark is a software protocol analyzer, or "packet sniffer" application. It is used for network troubleshooting, analysis, software and protocol development, and education. As data streams travel back and forth over the network, the sniffer "captures" each protocol data unit (PDU) and can decode and analyze its content according to the appropriate RFC or other specifications.

Wireshark is a useful tool for anyone working with networks and can be used for data analysis and troubleshooting with many of the labs in the networking courses. This lab provides instructions for downloading and installing Wireshark.

Required Resources

- 1 PC (Windows with internet access)

Instructions

Wireshark has become the industry standard packet-sniffer program used by network engineers. This open-source software is available for many different operating systems, including Windows, Mac, and Linux. In this lab, you will download and install the Wireshark software program on your PC.

Part 1: Download Wireshark

a. Wireshark can be downloaded from **www.wireshark.org**.

b. Click **Download** and choose the software version you need based on your PC's architecture and operating system. For instance, if you have a 64-bit PC running Windows, choose **Windows Installer (64-bit)**.

After making a selection, the download should start. The location of the downloaded file depends on the browser and operating system that you use. For Windows users, the default location is the **Downloads** folder.

Note: Wireshark recommends using the latest stable 3.6 release for 32-bit Windows.

Part 2: Install Wireshark

a. The downloaded file is named **Wireshark-win64-x.x.x.exe**, where **x** represents the version number. Double-click the file to start the installation process.

Respond to any security messages that may display on your screen. If you already have a copy of Wireshark on your PC, you will be prompted to uninstall the old version before installing the new version. It is recommended that you remove the old version of Wireshark prior to installing another version. Click **Yes** to uninstall the previous version of Wireshark.

b. You will see the Wireshark Setup wizard. Click **Next.**

c. Continue advancing through the installation process. Click **Noted** when the **License Agreement** window displays.

d. Keep the default settings in the **Choose Components** window and click **Next.**

e. Choose your desired shortcut options and click **Next.**

f. You can change the installation location of Wireshark, but unless you have limited disk space, it is recommended that you keep the default location. Click **Next** to continue.

g. To capture live network data, Npcap must be installed on your PC. If Npcap is already installed on your PC, the **Install** check box will be unchecked. If your installed version of Npcap is older than the version that comes with Wireshark, it is recommended that you allow the newer version to be installed by clicking the **Install Npcap x.x.x** (version number) checkbox. Click **Next** to continue.

h. **Do NOT** install USBPcap for normal traffic capture. **Do NOT select the checkbox to install USBPcap.** USBPcap is experimental, and it could cause USB problems on your PC. Click **Install** to continue.

i. Wireshark starts installing its files and displays the status of the installation.

j. In a separate window, accept the license agreement in the Npcap Setup Wizard if installing Npcap. Click **I Agree** to continue. Click **Install** to install Npcap. Click **Next** to finish the Npcap installation, and click **Finish** to exit the Npcap installation.

k. Click **Next** when the Wireshark installation is complete.

l. Click **Finish** to complete the Wireshark install process. Reboot the computer if necessary.

37.5.4 Lab–Use Network Tools to Learn About a Network

Figure 37-2   Topology

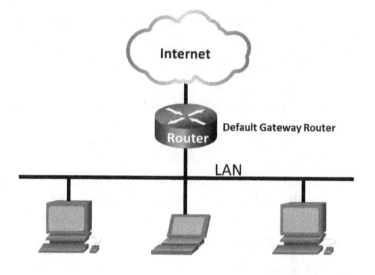

Objectives

- Part 1: Using Nmap (Optional)
- Part 2: Capture and Analyze Local ICMP Data in Wireshark
- Part 3: Capture and Analyze Remote ICMP Data in Wireshark

Background / Scenario

First, you will use the network scanning and mapping tool, Nmap, to discover hosts on your network. Nmap is a very popular network discovery and mapping tool that has many applications. You will then use the information gathered with Nmap to view network traffic in Wireshark.

Wireshark is a software protocol analyzer, or "packet sniffer" application, used for network troubleshooting, analysis, software and protocol development, and education. As data streams travel back and forth over the network, the sniffer "captures" each protocol data unit (PDU) and can decode and analyze its content according to the appropriate RFC or other specifications.

Wireshark is a useful tool for anyone working with networks and can be used with labs in the networking courses for data analysis and troubleshooting. In this lab, you will use Wireshark to capture ICMP data packet IP addresses and Ethernet frame MAC addresses.

Note: This lab can be done using a home network or in a networking learning lab with other students. The instructions will be slightly different depending on your setting.

Required Resources

- 1 PC (Windows with internet access)
- Additional PCs on a local-area network (LAN) will be used to reply to ping requests.

Instructions

Part 1: Using Nmap (Optional)

Note: This portion of the lab is optional. If you are doing this lab on your own, you will use Nmap to identify hosts on your network. If you are working with others, they will supply you with the IP addresses that you need to complete the Wireshark part of this lab. In some locations and environments, network scanning with a tool like Nmap is forbidden. **Only** use network scanning software on networks that you have explicit permission to scan.

Network Mapper (Nmap) is an open-source tool that allows you to scan IP addresses and ports in a network, discover services and open ports, and detect possible vulnerabilities. It is a good application to be familiar with, especially if you are interested in cybersecurity. You will use Nmap to identify devices on your local network by scanning your LAN.

Note: The following instructions are intended for Windows operating system only. Refer to the documentation at **https://nmap.org** for detailed information.

Step 1: Download and install Nmap.

a. Navigate to **https://nmap.org** and select the **Download** tab to download the latest Nmap stable installer for your system.

b. On your PC, navigate to the location of the downloaded file and double-click the file to start the installation process. Respond to any security messages that may display on your screen.

c. In the Nmap Setup wizard, click **I Agree** to accept the **License Agreement**.

d. Keep the default settings on the **Choose Components** window and click **Next**.

e. You can change the installation location of Nmap. Click **Install** to continue to install in the default **Destination** folder.

f. Click **Next** to create desired shortcuts. Click **Finish** to close the wizard after Nmap has successfully been installed on your computer.

Step 2: Learn more about Nmap.

a. The service **scanme.nmap.org** was set up by the Nmap Security Scanner Project to allow you to learn more about Nmap and verify that your Nmap installation is working properly.

   Nmap is often used as a command-line tool. In this lab, we will use Zenmap, the GUI version of Nmap.

b. Start **Nmap**. In the **Target** field in the Zenmap window, enter **scanme.nmap.org**. In the **Profile field**, select **Quick scan plus**. Click **Scan** to start a new scan.

c. The scan can take a few minutes. On the **Nmap Output** tab, you will see a small activity indicator next to the **executed Nmap command** dropdown and the **Details** button. This indicates that the scan is in progress. Review the results in the **Nmap Output** tab to answer a few questions.

   Questions:

   List some of the open ports.

What is the operating system is identified for the **scanme.nmap.org** server?

_____

What is the IP address for **scanme.nmap.org**?

_____

Step 3: Scan your home network.

For this lab, you will need to retrieve your PC IP address, subnet mask, and its network interface card (NIC) physical address, also called the MAC address.

a. In a command prompt window, enter **ipconfig /all** to determine the IP address of your PC interface, its description, and its MAC (physical) address.

```
C:\Users\Student> ipconfig /all

Windows IP Configuration

    Host Name . . . . . . . . . . . . : DESKTOP-NB48BTC
    Primary Dns Suffix  . . . . . . . :
    Node Type . . . . . . . . . . . . : Hybrid
    IP Routing Enabled. . . . . . . . : No
    WINS Proxy Enabled. . . . . . . . : No


Ethernet adapter Ethernet:

    Connection-specific DNS Suffix  . :
    Description . . . . . . . . . . . : Intel(R) 82577LM Gigabit
Network Connection
    Physical Address. . . . . . . . . :00-26-B9-DD-00-91
    DHCP Enabled. . . . . . . . . . . : No
    Autoconfiguration Enabled . . . . : Yes
    Link-local IPv6 Address . . . . . : fe80::d809:d939:110f:1b7f%20
(Preferred)
    IPv4 Address. . . . . . . . . . . : 192.168.1.147(Preferred)
    Subnet Mask . . . . . . . . . . . : 255.255.255.0
    Default Gateway . . . . . . . . . : 192.168.1.1
<output omitted>
```

b. Make note of the following:

- Interface name
- IP address
- Subnet mask
- Default gateway address
- Adapter physical address

c. Scan your computer by entering its IP address in the target window. Select the **Quick scan plus** profile and click **Scan**.

List some of the opened ports.

What is the operating system? Does the listed operating system match the operating system in use on the local host?

_____

d. You can also scan a subnet or entire IP network. To scan your local network, enter the IP address of your computer, followed by its subnet mask, in the **Target** field. The subnet mask should be in slash notation. For example, a mask of **255.255.255.0** is equivalent to **/24** in slash notation.

e. Select the Ping scan profile, because we just want a list of all the available hosts on the LAN. Click **Scan**.

Questions:

How many hosts were discovered? Was this number a surprise to you?

_____

With the Ping scan results, what other information is available to you?

_____

Try to identify which hosts were discovered based on the manufacturer information that is returned for the host NICs. This information comes from the MAC address's Organizational Unique Identifier (OUI). For more information, you can scan using the Quick Scan Plus or other profile. Can you identify some of the hosts?

_____

f. Make note of one or more IP addresses and the associated MAC addresses from the list.

Part 2: Capture and Analyze Local ICMP Data in Wireshark

In this part, you will ping another PC on the LAN and capture ICMP requests and replies in Wireshark. You will also look inside the frames captured for specific information. This analysis should help to clarify how packet headers are used to transport data to their destination.

Step 1: Retrieve your PC interface addresses.

If you have not done so already, determine the addressing information for your computer. You will need to retrieve your PC's IP address, subnet mask, and network interface card (NIC) physical address, also called the MAC address.

a. In a command prompt window, enter **ipconfig /all**, to the IP address of your PC interface, its description, and MAC (physical) address.

```
C:\Users\Student> ipconfig /all

Windows IP Configuration

    Host Name . . . . . . . . . . . . : DESKTOP-NB48BTC
    Primary Dns Suffix  . . . . . . . :
    Node Type . . . . . . . . . . . . : Hybrid
    IP Routing Enabled. . . . . . . . : No
    WINS Proxy Enabled. . . . . . . . : No
```

```
Ethernet adapter Ethernet:

   Connection-specific DNS Suffix   . :
   Description . . . . . . . . . . . : Intel(R) 82577LM Gigabit
Network Connection
   Physical Address. . . . . . . . . :00-26-B9-DD-00-91
   DHCP Enabled. . . . . . . . . . . : No
   Autoconfiguration Enabled . . . . : Yes
   Link-local IPv6 Address . . . . . : fe80::d809:d939:110f:1b7f%20
(Preferred)
   IPv4 Address. . . . . . . . . . . : 192.168.1.147(Preferred)
   Subnet Mask . . . . . . . . . . . : 255.255.255.0
   Default Gateway . . . . . . . . . : 192.168.1.1
<output omitted>
```

b. If you are working in a team, ask a team member for their PC IP address and provide your PC IP address to them. Do not provide them with your MAC address at this time.

If you are not permitted to scan the network with Nmap, you can use the default gateway for the next step.

Question:

Record the IP address you will use in the next step.

Step 2: Start Wireshark and begin capturing data.

a. Open Wireshark. Double-click the interface for your PC. The interface name should match the name in the ipconfig output. This will start the packet capture. Make sure the desired interface has traffic.

b. Information will start scrolling down the top section in Wireshark. The data lines will appear in different colors based on protocol. Each line contains information about a PDU that is travelling on the network.

This information can scroll by very quickly depending on what communication is taking place between your PC and the LAN. You can apply a filter to make it easier to view and work with the data being captured by Wireshark.

For this lab, we are only interested in displaying ICMP (ping) PDUs. Type **icmp** in the **Filter** box at the top of the Wireshark window and press **Enter**. You can also click the **Apply** button (arrow sign in the filter bar) to view only ICMP (ping) PDUs.

c. This filter causes all data in the top window to disappear, but you are still capturing the traffic on the interface. Navigate to a command prompt window and ping the IP address on another computer on the LAN. You obtained this address from either an Nmap scan or from a team member, if any. For example:

```
C:\> ping 192.168.1.114

Pinging 192.168.1.114 with 32 bytes of data:
Reply from 192.168.1.114: bytes=32 time<1ms TTL=128
Reply from 192.168.1.114: bytes=32 time<1ms TTL=128
```

```
Reply from 192.168.1.114: bytes=32 time<1ms TTL=128
Reply from 192.168.1.114: bytes=32 time<1ms TTL=128

Ping statistics for 192.168.1.114:
    Packets: Sent = 4, Received = 4, Lost = 0 (0% loss),
Approximate round trip times in milli-seconds:
    Minimum = 0ms, Maximum = 0ms, Average = 0ms
```

Notice that you start seeing data appear in Wireshark's top window again.

Figure 37-3   Capturing from Ethernet

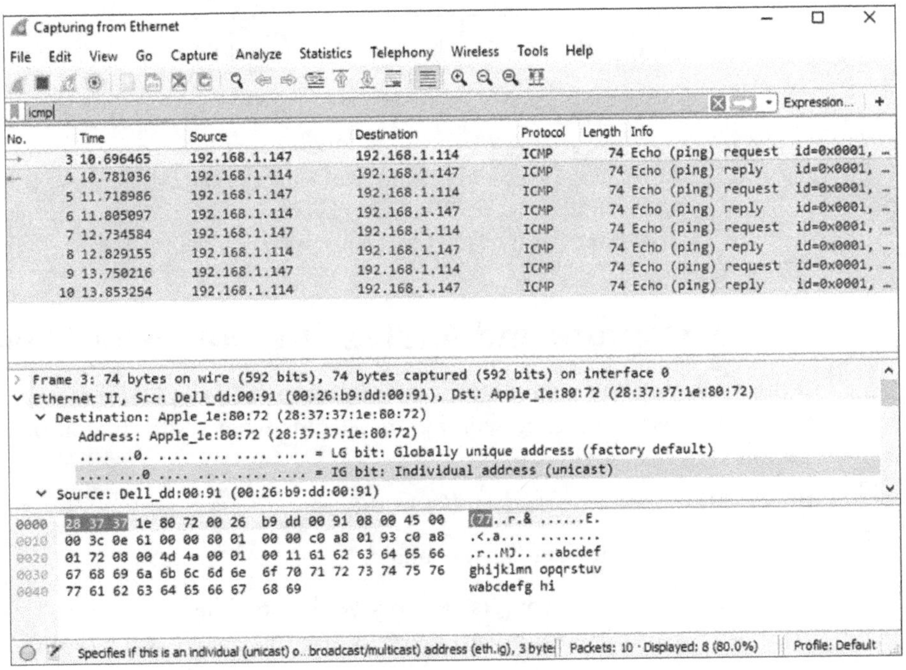

d. Stop capturing data by clicking the **Stop Capture** icon, which is the red square on the Wireshark toolbar.

Step 3: Examine the captured data.

Examine the data that was generated by the ping requests. Wireshark data is displayed in three sections:

1) The top section displays the list of PDU frames captured with a summary of the IP packet information listed

2) The middle section lists PDU information for the frame selected in the top part of the screen and separates a captured PDU frame by its protocol layers.

3) The bottom section displays the raw data of each layer.

a. Click the first ICMP request PDU frame in the top section of Wireshark. Notice that the **Source** column has your PC IP address, and the **Destination** column contains the IP address of the device that you pinged.

b. With this PDU frame still selected in the top section, navigate to the middle section. Click the arrow to the left of the Ethernet II row to view the destination and source MAC addresses.

Questions:

Does the source MAC address match your PC interface?

_____

Does the destination MAC address in Wireshark match your team member MAC address?

_____

How is the MAC address of the pinged PC obtained by your PC?

_____

Note: In the preceding example of a captured ICMP request, ICMP data is encapsulated inside an IPv4 packet PDU (IPv4 header), which is then encapsulated in an Ethernet II frame PDU (Ethernet II header) for transmission on the LAN.

Part 3: Capture and Analyze Remote ICMP Data in Wireshark

In this part, you will ping remote hosts (hosts not on the LAN) and examine the generated data from those pings. You will then determine what is different about this data from the data examined in the previous part.

Step 1: Start capturing data on the interface.

a. Start the data capture again.

b. A window prompts you to save the previously captured data before starting another capture. It is not necessary to save this data. Click **Continue without Saving**.

c. With the capture active, ping the following three website URLs from a Windows command prompt:

1) www.yahoo.com

2) www.cisco.com

3) www.google.com

Note: When you ping the URLs listed, notice that the Domain Name Server (DNS) translates the URL to an IP address. Note the IP address received for each URL.

d. You can stop capturing data by clicking the Stop Capture icon.

Step 2: Examining and analyzing the data from the remote hosts.

Review the captured data in Wireshark and examine the IP and MAC addresses of the three locations you pinged. List the destination IP and MAC addresses for all three locations in the space provided.

Questions:

What is the IP address for **www.yahoo.com**?

What is the MAC address for **www.yahoo.com?**

_____

What is the IP address for **www.cisco.com?**

_____

What is the MAC address for **www.cisco.com?**

_____

What is the IP address for **www.google.com?**

_____

What is the MAC address for **www.google.com?**

_____

What is significant about this information?

_____

How does this information differ from the local ping information you received in Part 2?

_____

Step 3: Save an open a packet capture file.

You can save the results of your Wireshark session in an external file. This file can then be opened in Wireshark to restore the session for analysis. This is a great way to archive network information and exchange scans with others.

a. Stop packet capture.

b. Go to the Wireshark file menu and select **Save**.

c. Name the file and choose a convenient location for the saved file.

d. You can open the file later by clicking the file menu and selecting **Open**.

Reflection Question

Why does Wireshark show the actual MAC address of the local hosts but not the actual MAC address for the remote hosts?

_____

Appendix A: Allowing ICMP Traffic Through a Firewall

If the members of your team cannot ping your PC, the firewall might be blocking those requests. This appendix describes how to create a rule in the firewall to allow ping requests. It also describes how to disable the new ICMP rule after you have completed the lab.

Part 1: Create a New Inbound Rule Allowing ICMP Traffic Through the Firewall

a. Navigate to the **Control Panel** and click the **System and Security** option in the **Category** view.

b. In the **System and Security** window, click **Windows Defender Firewall** or **Windows Firewall**.

c. In the left pane of the **Windows Defender Firewall** or **Windows Firewall** window, click **Advanced settings**.

d. On the **Advanced Security** window, click the **Inbound Rules** option on the left sidebar and then click **New Rule** on the right sidebar. This launches the **New Inbound Rule** wizard.

e. On the **Rule Type** screen, click the **Custom** radio button and click **Next**.

f. In the left pane, click the **Protocol and Ports** option, and using the **Protocol Type** drop-down menu, select **ICMPv4** and click **Next**.

g. Verify that **Any IP address** for both the local and remote IP addresses are selected. Click **Next** to continue.

h. Select **Allow the connection**. Click **Next** to continue.

i. By default, this rule applies to all the profiles. Click **Next** to continue.

j. Name the rule with **Allow ICMP Requests**. Click **Finish** to continue. This new rule should allow your team members to receive ping replies from your PC.

Part 2: Disabling or Deleting the New ICMP Rule

After the lab is complete, you may want to disable or even delete the new rule you created in Step 1. Using the **Disable Rule** option allows you to enable the rule again at a later date. Deleting the rule permanently deletes it from the list of inbound rules.

a. On the **Advanced Security** window, click **Inbound Rules** in the left pane and then locate the rule you created previously.

b. Right-click the ICMP rule and select **Disable Rule** if so desired. You may also select **Delete** if you want to permanently delete it. If you choose this option, you must re-create the rule to allow ICMP replies.

37.5.6 Packet Tracer–Troubleshooting Challenge–Use Documentation to Solve Issues

Addressing Table

Device	Interface	Device Type (router, switch, host)	IP Address	Subnet Mask	Default Gateway
PC1					
PC2					
PC3					
PC4					
PC5					
PC6					
PC7					

Objectives

In this lab, you use network documentation to identify and fix network communications problems.

- Use various techniques and tools to identify connectivity issues.
- Use documentation to guide troubleshooting efforts.
- Identify specific network problems.
- Implement solutions to network communication problems.
- Verify network operation.

Background / Scenario

In this activity, you will use the documentation that you created in the **Packet Tracer–Troubleshooting Challenge–Document the Network** activity to guide network troubleshooting efforts.

It has been discovered that the network that you worked with in the previous PT activity has developed communication problems. Some hosts cannot ping other hosts and the internet server. It is your job to determine what the issues are and to locate and repair them.

Network issues could exist in any device. Be sure to check for comprehensive errors:

- Addressing configuration
- Interface activation
- Routing
- NAT

Instructions

Passwords for all devices are VTY: **cisco**, Enable secret: **class**

Part 1: Assess Connectivity

All hosts should be able to ping each other and the internet server. Determine if this requirement is met. If not, identify which hosts and networks should be further investigated.

Part 2: Access Network Devices

From the hosts with communication problems, use ICMP tools to determine where these problems may be located in the network. From the host PCs, access devices in the network and display configurations and operational status.

Part 3: Repair the Network

After locating the issues, reconfigure the devices to repair the connectivity problem. Use your documentation from the previous activity to help you.

Part 4: Document the Issues

Record your issues in the table below.

Device	Issue	Action

CHAPTER 38

Cybersecurity Threats, Vulnerabilities, and Attacks

38.2.11 Lab–Explore Social Engineering Techniques

Objectives

- Part 1: Explore Social Engineering Techniques
- Part 2: Create a Cybersecurity Awareness Poster

Introduction

Cybersecurity is critical because it involves protecting unauthorized access to sensitive data, personally identifiable information (PII), protected health information (PHI), personal information, intellectual property (IP), and sensitive systems. Social engineering is a broad range of malicious activities accomplished by psychologically manipulating people into performing actions or divulging confidential information. In this lab, you will explore social engineering techniques, sometimes called human hacking, which is a broad category for different types of attacks.

Required Resources

PC or mobile device with internet access

Background / Scenario

Recent research reveals that the most common types of cyberattacks are becoming more sophisticated, and the attack targets are growing. The purpose of an attack is to steal information, disable systems or critical services, and disrupt systems, activities, and operations. Some attacks are designed to destroy information or information systems, maliciously control a computing environment or its infrastructure, or destroy the integrity of data and/or information systems. One of the most effective ways an attacker can gain access to an organization's network is through simple deception. In the cybersecurity world, this is called social engineering.

Social Engineering Attacks

Social engineering attacks are very effective because people want to trust other people, and social engineering attacks are not the kind of attack that the average user guards against; users are concerned with botnets, identity theft, or ransomware. These are big external threats, so they do not think to question what seems to be a legitimate-looking message.

Baiting

Baiting relies on the victim's curiosity or greed. What distinguishes baiting from other types of social engineering is the promise of an item or good that hackers use to entice victims. Baiters may offer users free music or movie downloads if the users surrender their login credentials to a certain site. Baiting attacks are not restricted to online schemes. Attackers can exploit human curiosity with physical media like USB drives.

Shoulder Surfing

Shoulder surfing is looking over someone's shoulder to get information. It is an effective way to get information in crowded places because it is relatively easy to stand next to someone and watch as they fill out a form or enter a PIN number at an ATM machine. It can also be done long distance with the aid of modern cell phones, binoculars, or other vision-enhancing devices. To prevent shoulder surfing, experts recommend that you shield paperwork or your keypad from view by using your body or cupping your hand. There are even screen shields that make shoulder surfing much more difficult.

Pretexting

Pretexting is using deception to create a scenario to convince victims to divulge information they should not divulge. Pretexting is often used against organizations that retain client data, such as financial data, credit card numbers, utilities account numbers, and other sensitive information. Pretexters often request information from individuals in an organization by impersonating a supervisor, helpdesk clerk, or client, and are usually conducted by phone, email, or text.

Phishing, spear phishing, and whaling attacks

In phishing attacks, the attackers try to obtain personal information or data, like usernames, passwords, and credit card details, by disguising themselves as trustworthy entities. Phishing is mainly conducted through emails and phone calls. Spear phishing is a more targeted version of phishing attacks in which an attacker chooses specific individuals or enterprises and then customizes their phishing attack to their victims to make it less conspicuous. Whaling is when the specific target is a high-profile employee such as a CEO or CFO.

Scareware and ransomware

Ransomware attacks involve injecting malware that encrypts a victim's critical data. The cyber criminals request a ransom to be paid to decrypt the data. However, even if a ransom is paid, there is no guarantee the cybercriminals will decrypt the information. Ransomware is one of the fastest growing types of cyberattack and has affected thousands of financial organizations, government agencies, healthcare facilities, and even schools and our education systems.

Scareware takes advantage of a user's fear by coaxing them into installing fake antivirus software.

Tailgating

Tailgating tricks the victim into helping the attacker gain unauthorized access into the organization's physical facilities. The attacker seeks entry into a restricted area where access is controlled by software-based electronic devices or human guards. Tailgating can also involve the attacker following an employee closely to pass through a locked door before the door locks behind the employee.

Dumpster diving

In the world of social engineering, dumpster diving is a technique used to retrieve discarded information thrown in the trash to carry out an attack on a person or organization. Dumpster diving is not limited to searching through the trash for obvious treasures such as access codes or passwords written down on sticky notes. It can also involve electronic information left on desktops, or stored on USB drives.

Instructions

Part 1: Explore Social Engineering Techniques

Step 1: Explore Baiting, Shoulder Surfing, and Pretexting

The National Support Center for Systems Security and Information Assurance (CSSIA) hosts a Social Engineering Interactive activity. The current link to the site is **https:// www.cssia.org/social_engineering/**. However, if the link changes, try searching for **CSSIA Social Engineering Interactive.**

Click **Next** in the interactive activity, and then use the content to answer the following questions.

Questions:

What is baiting? Did you click the USB drive? What happened to the victim's system?

_____

What is Shoulder Surfing? What device was used to perform the shoulder surfing? What information was gained?

_____

What is Pretexting? What type of information did the cybercriminal request? Would you fall victim?

_____

Step 2: Explore Phishing/Spear Phishing and Whaling

Phishing is designed to get victims to click links to malicious websites, open attachments containing malware, or revealing sensitive information. Use the interactive activity to explore different phishing techniques.

Questions:

In this phishing example, what is the ploy the attacker uses to trick the victim to visit the trap website? What is the trap website used to do?

_____

What is the difference between phishing and spear phishing or whaling?

_____

Step 3: Explore Scareware and Ransomware

Scareware is when victims are deceived into thinking their system is infected with malware and receive false alarms prompting them to install software that is not needed or is malware. Ransomware is a type of malware that threatens to publish the victim's data or encrypts the victim's data preventing access or the ability to use the data. Victims are prevented from accessing their system or personal files until they make a ransom payment to regain access.

Questions:

What data does the attacker claim to have in this example? Would you fall for this deception?

_____

What is the attacker requesting the victim do to get the data back?

_____

What is tailgating?

_____

Give three ways to prevent social engineering attacks?

_____

Part 2: Create a Cybersecurity Awareness Poster

Use Powerpoint to create a poster that will make others aware of the different social engineering techniques used to gain unauthorized access to an organization or the organization's data.

Pick from baiting, shoulder surfing, pretexting, phishing, scareware, ransomware, tailgating, or dumpster diving.

The poster should depict the techniques used and how users can avoid one of these social engineering attacks. Also, include directions on where the poster should be placed in the organization.

CHAPTER 39

Network Security

39.2.13 Packet Tracer–Configure Access Control

Objectives

- Part 1: Configure and Use AAA Authentication Credentials
- Part 2: Configure and Use Email Services
- Part 3: Configure and Use FTP Services

Background / Scenario

Authentication and authorization are distinct security processes in the world of identity and access management (IAM). Authentication uses passwords and other identification methods to confirm that users are who they say they are. By contrast, authorization assigns user permissions to the resources that the user is allowed access. In this Packet Tracer (PT) activity, you will configure authentication and authorization for network services including wireless network access, email, and FTP services.

Note: This activity opens in **Physical** mode. However, you can also complete it in **Logical** mode.

Note: Most tasks in this activity are graded. Click **Check Results** at any time to view your correct and incorrect Assessment Items.

Instructions

Part 1: Configure and Use AAA Authentication Credentials

Step 1: Configure user accounts on the AAA server.

a. Navigate to **Headquarters** and click the **Wiring Closet**, which is the tall, black server chassis in the bottom-left corner.

b. On the right side **Rack**, click **AAA-RADIUS** server > the **Services** tab, and then **AAA** under **Services**.

c. Enable the AAA service.

d. Under **User Setup**, add the following **usernames / passwords**.

- user1 / PASSuser1!
- user2 / PASSuser2!

Step 2: Configure wireless authentication on HQ-Laptop-1.

a. Navigate back to **HQ** and click **HQ-Laptop-1**, located two rooms to the right from the Wiring Closet.

b. Click the **Config** tab, and then under **Interface**, click **Wireless0**.

c. In the SSID box, type **HQ-INT**.

d. In the **Authentication** area, click **WPA2**.

e. In the **User ID** box, enter **user1**, and enter **PASSuser1!** in the **Password** box.

f. In the **IP Configuration** section, click **DHCP**. Wait a few moments for the DHCP offer to be accepted. Verify that **HQ-Laptop-1** received the IP addressing and is assigned an address on the 192.168.50.0/24 network.

Note: It might be necessary to toggle between **Static** and **DHCP** to force Packet Tracer to converge on your settings. Also, click **Check Results** to make sure you correctly configured the AAA server and the wireless settings on the laptop. Clicking **Check Results** may also force Packet Tracer to converge. If everything is configured correctly, proceed to the configuration of **HQ-Laptop-2**, and then return to **HQ-Laptop-1** and check its IP configuration. This issue is typically resolved.

Step 3: Configure wireless authentication on HQ-Laptop-2.

a. Click **HQ-Laptop-2**, which is located in the top-right corner of **HQ**.

b. Repeat the previous steps to configure the wireless settings for **HQ-Laptop-2**, using the **user2** credentials.

c. Verify that **HQ-Laptop-2** received the IP addressing and is assigned an address on the 192.168.50.0/24 network.

Part 2: Configure and Use Email Services

Step 1: Activate email services and configure email user accounts.

a. Navigate to the **Wiring Closet**.

b. On the right side **Rack**, click **Mail** server > **Services** tab, and then **Email** under **Services**.

c. Turn on both the **SMTP** and **POP3** services.

d. Set the domain to **mail.cyberhq.com**.

e. Under **User Setup**, enter the following **usernames / passwords**. Click the plus sign (**+**) to add each pair.

- HQuser1 / Cisco123!
- HQuser2 / Cisco123~
- BRuser1 / Cisco123-
- BRuser2 / Cisco123+

Step 2: Configure email clients.

a. Navigate back to **HQ** and click the **PC 1-1** in the bottom corner.

b. Click the **Desktop** tab and select **Email**. The **Configure Mail** settings open.

c. Enter the following information:

- Your Name: **Suk-Yi**
- Email Address: **HQuser1@mail.cyberhq.com**
- Incoming & Outgoing Email Server(s): **mail.cyberhq.com**
- User Name: **HQuser1**
- Password: **Cisco123!**

d. Click **Save**.

e. Use the information in the table to configure email settings for **2-3**, **HQ-Laptop-1**, and **Net-Admin**. PC **2-3** is in the office below the conference room. The **Net-Admin** PC is in the **Wiring Closet**.

PC / Laptop	Your Name	Email address	User Name	Password
2-3	Ajulo	BRuser1@mail.cyberhq.com	BRuser1	Cisco123-
HQ-Laptop-1	Malia	BRuser2@mail.cyberhq.com	BRuser2	Cisco123+
Net-Admin	Cisco	HQuser2@mail.cyberhq.com	HQuser2	Cisco123~

Step 3: Send an email as Suk-Yi.

a. On PC **1-1**, click **Compose**.

b. Compose an email to Ajulo at **BRuser1@mail.cyberhq.com**. Enter a subject and email message of your choice. Click **Send** when finished.

Note: Packet Tracer may take several seconds to converge before you see a **Send Success** message at the bottom of the window.

Note: Packet Tracer does not grade this step. Verify you correctly completed this step by receiving the email sent by Suk-Yi on Ajulo's PC **2-3**.

c. Navigate to Ajulo's PC **2-3**. If necessary, click the **Desktop** tab and select **Email**.

d. Click **Receive** and read the email from Suk-Yi.

Part 3: Configure and Use FTP Services

Step 1: Activate the FTP Service.

a. Navigate to the **Wiring Closet**.

b. On the right side **Rack**, click **FTP** server, and on the **Services** tab, choose **FTP** under **Services**.

c. Turn on the **FTP** service.

Step 2: Create the FTP user accounts.

a. Under **User Setup**, enter the following usernames, passwords, and privileges. Click **Add** to add each user.

Note: Be sure username **malia** does not include **Delete** as one of the user privileges.

Username	Password	User Privilege
sukyi	cisco123	RWDNL (Write, Read, Delete, Rename, List)
ajulo	cisco321	RWDNL (Write, Read, Delete, Rename, List)
malia	cisco123	RWNL (Write, Read, Rename, List)

b. Verify each user is correctly created, and close the server.

Step 3: Transfer files between Net-Admin and the FTP server.

a. Click **Net-Admin** PC, and then click **Desktop > Command Prompt**.

b. Enter the **ftp 192.168.75.2** command to log in to the FTP server, and then authenticate with username **sukyi** and password **cisco123**.

c. Enter the **dir** command to list the files on the FTP server.

d. Use the **get** command to download **aMessage.txt**.

e. Quit the FTP session.

f. Close the **Command Prompt**, click **Text Editor**, and then choose **File > Open**. Open the downloaded file **aMessage.txt**.

Question:

What is the message in the file?

_____

g. Click **File > New**. Type a text message.

h. Click **File > Save** and save the new file as **aMessage_new.txt**. Close the **Text Editor**.

i. Click **Command Prompt** and log in to the FTP server as user **sukyi**.

j. Use the **put** command to upload **aMessage_new.txt**.

k. Quit the FTP session.

Step 4: Verify FTP user privileges are working as configured.

a. Navigate back to **HQ** and click **HQ-Laptop-1**, select the **Desktop** tab, and choose **Command Prompt**.

b. Log in to the FTP server at 192.168.75.2 with username **malia** and password **cisco123**.

c. Use the **delete** command to attempt to remove the newly uploaded file, **aMessage_new.txt**.

Question:

Were you able to delete file from the FTP server? Explain.

_____

d. Use the **rename** command to attempt to change the **aMessage_new.txt** name to **aMessage_rename.txt**.

```
ftp> rename aMessage_new.txt aMessage_rename.txt
```

Question:

Were you able to rename file from the FTP server?

_____

e. Quit the FTP session, and close the **HQ-Laptop-1** window.

Packet Tracer
☐ Activity

39.6.16 Packet Tracer–Configure Basic Wireless Security

Objectives

- Configure basic wireless security using WPA2 Personal.

Background / Scenario

A small business owner learns that the wireless network should be secured from unauthorized access. He has decided to use WPA2 Personal for his network.

Instructions

Part 1: Verify Connectivity

a. On the laptop, choose Desktop > Web Browser.

b. Enter **www.cisco.pka** as the URL. The web page should display.

Part 2: Configure Basic Wireless Security

a. Enter **192.168.1.1** in the web browser to access the wireless router. Enter **admin** as the username and password.

b. Click the **Wireless** menu. Select the **Wireless Security** menu.

c. The security mode is disabled currently. For the 2.4 GHz network, change the security mode to **WPA2 Personal**. For the 5 GHz networks, you can leave them disabled.

d. In the **Passphrase** field, enter **Network123**.

e. Scroll down to the bottom of the page and click **Save Settings**. Close the web browser.

Part 3: Update the Wireless Settings on Laptop

a. Click **PC Wireless** on the **Desktop** tab.

b. Click the **Connect** tab. Select the **Academy** and click **Connect**.

c. Enter **Network123** as the pre-shared key. Click **Connect**.

d. Close the **PC Wireless** window.

Part 4: Verify Connectivity

a. Access the **Web Browser**.

b. Enter **www.cisco.pka** as the URL. Verify that the web page displays after the addition of the basic wireless configuration.

c. If you cannot access the web page, verify your wireless settings on the wireless router and the laptop. Also, verify that laptop is connected to the wireless router.